I0764670

HB

ALSO AVAILABLE FROM HANS BEUMER:

THE GLOBAL TRAVELLER SERIES:

20,000 KM BY TRAIN

Visit www.hansbeumer.com

THE ULTIMATE HAPPINESS SERIES:

TRAVEL GUIDE TO SELF-ACTUALIZATION

by Hans Beumer

Hans Beumer Publications
2016

Hans Beumer Publications
Feldpark 29
6300 Zug
Switzerland

First edition published in April 2016:
ISBN 978-3-906861-04-3 (US Trade Paperback Color)

This book is also available as:
-US Trade Paperback (B/W): ISBN 978-3-906861-05-0
-EBook: ISBN 978-3-906861-06-7

Typeset body text in Garamond 11.5
Printed and distributed by Lulu Press, Inc.

www.hansbeumer.com

*To travel is to leave behind your past baggage,
and refill your baggage with new content,
of experiences, reflections and outlooks*

A sincere thanks to Audrey
for accompanying and supporting me
during the travel to the purpose of my life

Contents

Foreword

This is the first book of *'The Ultimate Happiness Series'*. Books published under this Series provide you guidance for finding enduring happiness. The Series help you develop your own happiness as a result of which you will improve your own life, the lives of the people around you and society at large.

The book is set in Thailand because of its warm climate during Winter time, the friendliness of the local people, the relatively low cost of living and the stunning locations, cultural heritages and beaches. It is a non-fiction novel and describes actual people and actual events. It narrates experiences and activities, people, sightseeing, travelling and the locations of three months overwintering in Thailand. From this perspective, this book is a combination of a story about spiritual development for finding the purpose in life and a travel journal.

I hope that this book inspires you to find the purpose of your life, so that you soon reach your Ultimate Happiness level, and through your own purpose, support humankind in improving the life of other people. The world will be such a better and happier place when everybody is fulfilling the purpose of his/her life.

Read to advance your life,

drs. Hans Beumer
April 2016

Step 1

Introducing the Purpose of Life

Do you struggle in your daily existence and never have that feeling of excitement that what you are doing is meaningful for yourself and others? Most of us live a life in a daily routine, which focuses on the obligation to work, taking care of family, satisfying financial obligations, etc. How are you going to find "the meaning of your life"? You need to find meaning within your existing daily life. And that is possible, because it is fully under your own control to shape your daily life. You are not in a straight jacket; there are always alternatives, as long as you have the courage to seek, decide and follow through on those.

The pathway is not about becoming a hermit, and spending 3 years, 3 months, 3 weeks, 3 days, and 3 hours meditating in a cave.
It is not about disavowing all earthly goods and benefits, and becoming a monk and contemplating the rest of your life in prayers.
It should not be a pathway that only finds meaning in the afterlife, after death, for example through the belief of going to heaven or achieving nirvana (and suffer during a life-time to get there).
The pathway is independent from the path you walked in the past: if you did not find meaning in the past: no problem, it can always change. According to your consciousness, we live in the now, not in the future, nor in the past. Your consciousness is only aware of the here and now.

Improving the Life of Other People

Leading a purposeful life generally means positively contributing to the life of others. What do you need to do for another person? When making decisions on a daily basis, you could keep in mind the question: will this bring happiness to others? But this is a difficult question to answer for each individual, as happiness of another person is determined in the mind of that other person. The concept of happiness is difficult to define and measure. A more straightforward concept is to contribute to the advancement of another person on his/her way to leading a purposeful life. This is easier to define and measure, and can be somewhat assessed by the person that provides the contribution. It is this advancement that should result in happiness for that other person.

This book is about finding your life's goal. Find your passion in life and pursue that. At this level, the passion should relate to a cause greater than oneself. It should be for the benefit of others. When you find such purpose, your life will become much easier and far more rewarding. It will probably need risk taking to get out of your comfort zone and identify your true purpose in life. But when you wake up every morning full of energy and exhilaration, then you know that you are on the right path. This is the ultimate purpose of life: your contribution to the advancement of others. And when you improve the lives of others, you elevate your own life at the same time. The world would be such a better place when everybody would be fulfilling the purpose of his/her life.

So the question becomes, how to generate a lasting positive impact on the lives of others. The question is easily posed, but the answer might be difficult to find. Also, the answer might shift during your lifetime. Usually a person goes through several stages during his/her lifetime. At present you are most likely in one of the following stages: being educated in your early years, developing your career, raising and taking care of your family, maturing in your career or retiring in your late years. Quite often during each of these stages you are following specific stage-related objectives, which fulfill the purpose of your life in that specific stage. Your transition from one stage to the next stage is the ideal time to reassess the purpose of your life.

Determine the purpose of your life to improve your own life, the lives of the people around you and society at large. This book shows how you can find the purpose of your life with the support of travelling. Travel to sort out your future. Travel to leave the past baggage behind and spiritually refill your bags with new experiences, reflections and outlooks. Travel to find Your Self.

Seven Simple Steps

This book provides concrete and practical guidance. There are no other books on the market which link the search for the purpose in life to conditions created during travel. Travel expands the experiences, tolerances and mind and spirit, it literally enables you to leave behind your existing life, at least from a geographical point of view. Travel will also enable you to leave behind your existing life from a spiritual point of view. This creates the conditions for the mind to be opened up for new thoughts. In order for the teacup to be filled with fresh and warm tea, it must first be emptied of the old and cold tea. Once your mind is opened up, your teacup emptied, you can enter into the second stage.

This book guides you through *Seven Simple Steps* to get from where you are today to fulfilling the purpose of your life. The Seven Simple Steps approach may lead to your Self-Actualization in less than three months nominal time. The approach is supported by travel, because travel takes you out of your daily environment and enables a refocus. Ken accomplished these Seven Simple Steps during one trip, three months overwintering in Thailand. But you might not have that much time available in one stretch. That is no hinder to achieving the Seven Simple Steps though. During Ken's trip, each step was linked to a specific location. So also you can link each step to a specific location that you want to travel to and complete a single step at that single location. You might even find a way to progress with the Seven Simple Steps in between your travels, while at home in your daily environment.

The Seven Simple Steps are:

1. Creating awareness that you have an existing situation that needs to be addressed, introducing the concept of the purpose of your life
2. Letting go of past baggage
3. Read up on your materials and take inventory
4. Relax and think to come to your vision
5. Expand your vision

6. Putting your vision to the test: laying the cornerstone for building the future
7. Start living the purpose of your life

Each of the Chapters guides you through the Seven Simple Steps. In order to make it easier for you, at the end of each Chapter several questions are raised to guide your self-refection. These are the points to contemplate and personalize.

Two Interwoven Story Lines

This book has two interwoven and linked story lines: the story of finding the purpose of life combined with the experiences of three months overwintering in Thailand at six locations including the most beautiful beaches.

The main character in this novel is called Ken. Ken is in his early 50s and recently quit his corporate job for a time of reflection and self-actualization. This is his story about overwintering for three months in Thailand, in the good company of his wife and best friend Julie. On 5th November 2015, Ken flew to Thailand for a three month stay. You will read how he was able to:
- alleviate the work stress of the past 30 years
- spiritually develop, think about life to find his passion and purpose of life, and decide the next steps after the three months
- give back to society

Six Locations in Thailand

This book describes six locations in Thailand: Bangkok, Ko Samui, Ko Phuket, Ko Phi Phi, Krabi and Ko Yao. Bangkok and Krabi are on the mainland; the four Ko's are Islands. This non-fiction novel includes descriptions of these locations as a well as a selection of the most interesting sights that were visited. The book includes travel experiences, which are supported by over 200 pictures visualizing the beautiful Thai locations. Each of the six locations plays their own role in achieving Ken's objectives. The descriptions of the roles of these six locations will clearly show the development that Ken goes through during the three months in Thailand. The developmental stages of his thought processes coincide with the changes in locations and each location provides its own contribution. Each location completes one step from the *Seven Simple Steps*.

In *Step 2* Ken visits Bangkok. Bangkok is central for exploring the Thai cultural heritage through sightseeing trips, which causes a high level of distraction from the work past. Exploring the new sites, smells and sounds and meeting the kind smiling warm-hearted people give a great boost to changing his state of mind. Read how he is able to let go of the baggage from the past.

In *Step 3* Ko Samui Island is visited. Because of the rainy weather, stinging insects and the limited sightseeing places on the island, Ken spends most of the days on the balcony of his room at the resort. Read how he is able to progress with reading and taking inventory of his life.

In *Step 4* he spends four weeks on Ko Phuket Island, where he mostly reads, thinks, writes and relaxes. It is because of the relaxing and thinking time during the long beach walks, that he receives the vision for his future life.

In *Step 5* Ko Phi Phi Island is described as a paradise-like setting. Read how Ken starts meditation to find silence and contemplates how to follow his passion. The trip on the long-tail boat to Phi Phi Ley Island is probably the best experience of the whole three months, and elevates his happiness to the highest level.

In *Step 6* Ken is back on the mainland, in Krabi. Read how he uses the five days at that location to lay the foundation for building his new purpose in life.

In *Step 7* Ken spends the last five days of the three months on Ko Yao. The serenity and tranquility are a climax in finishing three months in Thailand. Meditation and the environment are a highlight, inducing reading and thinking. Read how he is mentally prepared to follow his passion, and how he is spiritually ready to give back to society.

The final Chapters provide a *Summary* of the travel guide to Self-Actualization, followed by a summary of the *Seven Simple Steps* approach. The book is completed with a list of *Recommended Reading*, which will provide you different perspectives on the pathway to finding the purpose of your life.

Points to Contemplate and Personalize

Think about the following questions. Do this thinking in silence and without distractions. Take out a sheet of paper. Write down your thoughts as detailed as possible. Put the sheet of paper away for at least one night. Before you go to sleep, clear your mind and only contemplate these questions in your mind and ask your subconscious mind to provide guidance. Immediately after waking up the next morning, contemplate these questions and answers again. Do this in silence and without distractions. Take your sheet of paper and make any required adaptations to the answers. Ideally you should not go about this alone, so discuss the results with your life's partner or another person whom you deeply trust and rely on. Your life's partner may be able to give you an outside perspective and stimulate critical thinking. Repeat this process till you are satisfied with the results.

Key questions:

Do you know what the passion of your life is?
Do you improve the life of other people?
Do you struggle in your daily existence and never have that feeling of excitement that what you are doing is meaningful for yourself and others?
What part of your life would you like to change to give it meaning and passion?

Keep in mind:

Your life is under your full control, and if you don't like certain aspects of your life, it is up to you to initiate the changes.
The answers to these questions usually have a high correlation to the stage of your life, unless you are in a transition from one stage to the next.

Your progress:

Your contemplation and personalization of these topics round off step one from the Seven Simple Steps. You have now created awareness that you have an existing situation that needs to be addressed. You understand the concept of the purpose of your life and why it matters that you fulfill the purpose of your life.

Step 2

Bangkok:
Letting go of Past Baggage

It is Friday sixth of November 2015 and after only a few hours of sleep Ken wakes up in the uncomfortable position of the economy class seat. He has another three hours of flight to go and watches movies to kill time, while he waits for breakfast to be served. Outside it is already light, but with all the shutters closed, the cabin is dark. It is warm in the cabin; no blanket or sweater is needed. The airplane touches down at Bangkok's Suvarnabhumi airport at 10 a.m. local time. Disembarking is slow. Immigration is also slow with long queues. Julie goes first when they arrive at the front of the queue. The immigration officer while checking Julie's passport is distracted by a colleague talking to him. When it is Ken's turn, he asks him whether he and Julie are together. After a yes answer, he calls Julie back, as she had already walked on towards the baggage area. Apparently he forgot to register her visa. At luggage belt 18 Ken finds the two aluminum Rimowa suitcases already on the belt. He changes $100 for Baht in order to have cash for the taxi. After passing through customs he quickly finds the taxi area. He walks over to a row of taxis but gets sent back because he doesn't have a ticket, which shows the corresponding number to the parking place number of the taxi. Ken takes a look at the booth of the small size taxis and concludes that the two large cases need a big size taxi. At the taxi ticket machine he draws a stub with a number where big size taxis stand. The taxi ride to the JW Marriott Bangkok hotel takes 40 minutes through dense but moving traffic.

JW Marriott Bangkok

Ken checks in, and at the counter the Thai lady is surprised that he and his wife are staying for so long, 25 nights. She gives them a quiet room, away from the elevator and street. The hotel and room interiors at the JW Marriott are nice. Julie unpacks their suitcases and finds out that the closet is too small. It isn't really suitable for two people staying for 25 nights. Early afternoon Ken feels so tired from the uncomfortable night in the airplane seat that he can't resist the temptation to lie down on the soft and fresh bed, where he can stretch and lie flat. His eyelids quickly close, and his mind floats away in an undisturbed and deep sleep. By early evening, Ken forces himself to wake up. After a quick fresh up, Ken and Julie leave the room to check out the hotel restaurants. The hotel offers Japanese, Chinese, NY steakhouse and international food. They sit down at the hotel's international restaurant. Ken decides for the buffet, which offers a wide variety of choice and offers excellent taste.

The next morning it seems that all Ken did yesterday was sleep. And he still needs to force himself to wake up. His biorhythm is still in the time zone of his home country. He freshens up and goes down for breakfast. It is a large buffet with a lot of choice and good quality of food, ranging from Indian, Chinese, Japanese, freshly made pancakes and omelets to salads, breads, fruits and freshly squeezed juices. Ken has a fresh cappuccino, muesli with yoghurt and egg and toast. Breakfast is till 10:30 a.m., so they are in no hurry, and Ken reads the local Bangkok paper while enjoying a second cappuccino. Back in their room on the 15th floor, Ken changes into his swimming trunks. On the 6th floor of the hotel there is a large Spa, Gym and Pool area, where Ken and Julie spend the afternoon. It is warm, 32 degrees Celsius, with a moderate level of humidity, while skies are cloudy. They lie on a sun chair close to the pool, where Ken relaxes with a book titled "What makes you not a Buddhist". After the cold at home, the warm air and the sunrays on their skin feel so good, reloading the shortage of natural vitamin D. As the hotel's outdoor pool area is on the sixth floor and surrounded by high buildings, early afternoon the sun disappears and is replaced by shade. Fortunately Ken stays wrapped in the blanket of warm air, even after the sunrays can't touch him anymore. The book that Ken is reading makes him think about the purpose of his life. So before leaving the pool area, he debates with Julie about the spiritual topics and philosophies of the book. As the evening's darkness approaches, Ken and Julie go back to their room to shower and get dressed. The couple wants to try different food and walk out to the mall across the street. This mall is rather small, but it contains a McDonalds and a Starbucks. The three local restaurants don't offer much. As they are hungry and don't want to wonder off to find something else, the decision is quickly made in favor of a Lebanese restaurant. They cross the street and stroll back to their hotel through the darkness.

JW Marriott Bangkok — Pool area

Fitness at Hotel — Room 1035

Thai Entertainment

After a brief visit to their room, they go down to the lobby where Ken asks the concierge for a map of Bangkok. The concierge points out a close by entertainment area, with bars, restaurants and clubs. It's just a five-minute walk around two corners. The street is packed with open bars, where loud music greets the pedestrians and slim Thai girls (or boys dressed and looking like girls) inviting the passing (mostly) single-white-males in their

20s to 50s to come in and have a drink. Between the open bars are massage parlors, where the girls sit in a row waiting to be chosen to give the massage, and small stores selling fake brand wallets, bags, etc. On the street side of the walkway there are small stalls where vendors sell their food, like fried fish, satay, soup, noodles, fried insects, etc. The sewage smells mix with the smells of the food stalls, together under a warm blanket of high humidity. Ken enters an area for adult entertainment, where a three-story building around a central courtyard, houses many pole-dancing clubs. When Ken takes a peek behind the curtains at one of the entrances he sees the formerly mentioned single white males sitting on the side, while slim and young Thai girls (or maybe boys, who knows) are dancing in their underwear in the center of the room. Behind another curtain Ken observes two topless Thai girls dancing in a bathtub while foaming each other. Many girls are standing in the corridors and try to lure him into their club. Not surprisingly, Julie does not get much attention. The couple decides to leave the courtyard and walk to another street, which turns out to be the Arabic area. There are no loud bars, but instead many Arabic restaurants, men and women in long dress, incense and other Arabic shops. The walkway has a plastic overhead cover between the shops and the booths of the street vendors. They sell fake branded bags, wallets, sports goods, watches, etc. Because of the overhead plastic cover all heat is trapped inside this walkway, making it unbearable for them to continue browsing around. After walking around for some time, Ken finds the way back to the hotel, and the couple is relieved to be in their room with the cool air-conditioning.

Street Food

Street Scene

Yoga, Fitness, Cardio, Muay Thai

That night, Ken wakes up at 2 a.m. and it takes long for him to fall asleep again. As a consequence he struggles to wake up at 9:30 a.m., which is necessary to ensure that he can still make it for breakfast, which closes at 10:30 a.m. It is crowded at the breakfast restaurant, as many tourists as well as local people enjoy the weekend at the hotel. Later at the pool area it is easy to find two sun chairs; not many people are there. With the sun shining through the clouds, it is hot immediately, and Ken moves to a place under a roof in the shade. He catches up with writing the travel journal and reading. He writes a daily travel journal to keep his children, parents, family and friends back home up-to-date. In the afternoon he joins the hotel's Boot Camp fitness class. During 45 minutes he huffs and puffs and sweats while doing exercises for legs and abs in a group of five, with an instructor called Chati. Subsequently, Ken trains in the gym. The hotel gym is large and fully equipped, and well maintained. Back at the room Ken changes his sweaty sports clothing for swimming wear and goes back to the pool. He has a protein shake from the fitness bar and completes the blogs on his MacBook. When leaving the pool, the menu at the fitness bar catches his eye. They offer light and healthy food for a fair price. So Ken and Julie go there for dinner. Ken has Caesar salad with grilled shrimps while Julie orders Salmon with Spinach. Both dishes taste great.

Ken lies awake from 2 till 4 a.m. as he struggles with the time difference. He needs the alarm to be woken up on time in order to still make it for breakfast. Last night Ken talked to the front desk about changing their room to a more spacious one. The room is too small with too little storage capacity for their clothing. The room is suitable for a few days stay, but they are carrying clothing and shoes for three months. So the front desk arranged a new room. After breakfast Ken leaves the packed cases in the room, drops off the room key at the front desk and goes to the pool to relax and read. Early afternoon he picks up the new room key for room nr. 1035. When they check into the new room, their luggage is already there. The room is double the size of their previous room, with a walk-in closet. They are happy with the increased space and immediately feel at home in the room. After they unpack, it is time for sports again. Ken and Julie change into their sports attire and do an hour of Yoga class. It is the very first time that they do Yoga. According to them, it is comparable to one long session of continued painful stretching. They are so inflexible, making their first encounter with Yoga quite tough. The Thai Yoga teacher immediately sees that they are new to this, compared to the four other participants. Ken laughs at himself, because the positions of the limbs and body seem impossible, and all muscles are stretched to the threshold of pain. At the end of the session the group spends 15 minutes lying in the dark, while the Thai teacher moves from person to person to give each a short back massage. It was tough but felt pretty good to Ken. Early dinner is at the fitness bar, consisting of a club sandwich, after which they relax at the pool. After having digested the food, Ken takes the 45 minutes Body Toning class in the early evening. The Thai teacher lets them train with lightweights for all muscle groups. It is intensive but not so heavy. Ken planned a third session of sports for that day, and after a short break, he joins the Muay Thai class for 45 minutes. This is Thai Kick Boxing, for which Ken puts on boxing gloves and removes his trainers and socks. Chati shows the newcomers eight basic moves, and lets them practice while he spars with three other Thai participants, who are a lot better and experienced at this. The boxing itself is okay, though the bones in the hand and wrist hurt from hitting the punching bag. Ken finds the leg kicks really difficult. He is not flexible enough to raise his leg straight and high, plus he needs to kick the punching bag with his shins, which is not a pleasant feeling. The hours of sports were exhausting, and his body is tired and aches. The hotel's Spa brings relief, as his body relaxes in the warm Jacuzzi, dry sauna and steam room. This was a super sports day, ending with relaxing and pampering of his strained muscles.

Grand Palace

Not surprisingly, Ken slept very well and had to be woken up by the alarm. The plan for today is to go sightseeing in Bangkok. But as they have run out of Baht currency, they need to exchange some more. Ken enquires at the front desk of the hotel for their rate, which turns out to be not as good as the rates he saw at the small currency exchange counters on the streets. So after breakfast he changes $300 to Baht at a small kiosk in a street close to the hotel. Having sufficient Baht again to pay for their local activities, Ken and Julie take a taxi to downtown Bangkok. It takes them there in 30 minutes for 100 Baht ($2.70). Taxis are cheap and comfortable, as they are air-conditioned in the hot and humid weather. They get out at the entrance of the Wat Phra Kaew (Temple of the Emerald Buddha) and Grand Palace complex, which is Bangkok's most important and exotic attraction. It was built in 1782 as the King's new palace for the new capital Bangkok, as well as a new residence to house the Emerald Buddha, the country's most revered religious image. For about two hours Ken and Julie walk around in the complex of temples, and mingle with the many other tourists. The temples are beautifully decorated with colored glass and gold. Ken takes many pictures of the buildings that sparkle in the sunlight. Inside most temples, however it is not allowed to take pictures. The dress code prescribes no bare legs or shoulders and shoes have to be taken off in most religious temples. But Ken came prepared for this; so in the long sleeves and pants he sweats away in 34 degrees Celsius, with a high level of humidity. For the return journey Ken needs to negotiate with several taxi drivers before he finds one that wants to use the meter. In 40 minutes they are back at the hotel, where the couple enjoys an early dinner at the fitness bar. Digestion takes place on the sun chair at the pool area. Early evening Ken does an hour cardio workout at the gym.

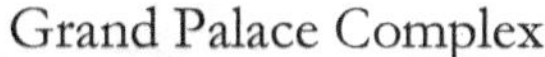

Grand Palace Complex

Wat Pho Temple

After breakfast at the hotel, Ken and Julie take a taxi to downtown Bangkok to visit the Wat Pho Temple complex, the cities' oldest temple, dating back to the 16th century. It houses a monumental reclining Buddha from the year 1832, that is 46 meters long and 15 meters high, depicting the Buddha passing into Nirvana, having achieved enlightenment. The cloisters contain almost 400 bronzes Buddha images retrieved from ancient ruins in Sukhothai and Ayutthaya. Ken admires the temples and statues for about two hours and takes many pictures. Although also this complex is crowded with tourists, there is more space here to move around without having to undergo penguin-like queues and pace. Also here Ken needs proper dress and shoes must be left outside the temples. The complex includes a Thai massage center/school, but Ken does not make use of that. For the return taxi they need to haggle with several drivers before Ken finds one for a reasonable price of 150 Baht ($4.30). Back at the hotel it is time for early dinner at the fitness bar and relaxation at the pool. Early evening it is time for Chati's Boot Camp class and after a 15-minute break, Ken continues with Tai Chi/Yoga class. That teacher is like a snake-woman. During an hour she shows many Tai-Chi movements of arms and balancing positions of the body, while she emphasizes controlled breathing. Ken tries to follow, but has difficulties copying the positions; he is so inflexible. He mostly neglects the breathing part, as he concentrates on the movements of arms while not losing his balance. For him it is basically one long stretching session. Ken laughs at how unable he is to follow the teacher, but afterwards he does feel good.

Wat Pho Temple Complex

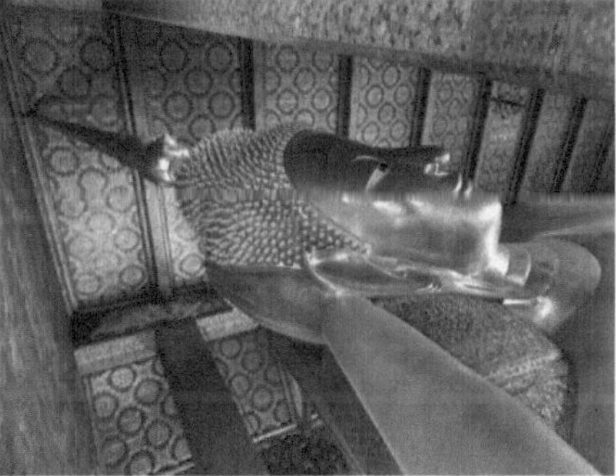

Bang Pa-In and Ayutthaya

Ken wakes up by the alarm at 7:30 a.m. in order to be able to leave early, as they want to undertake a trip outside of Bangkok. After breakfast Ken turns to the travel desk of the hotel for their advice how to travel to Ayutthaya, 85 kilometers North of Bangkok. After some discussion, Ken accepts their suggestion that one of their drivers takes them for 3,000 Baht ($85) for the five-hour trip. They are guided to the hotel parking garage, from where the car gets them out of Bangkok without much traffic. After 60 kilometers the driver makes a stop at Bang Pa-In, which is a collection of pavilions and palaces in Thai, European and Chinese style, once used as a royal summer retreat. Most of the buildings are closed to the public, so they can only visit a few buildings, where it is not allowed to take pictures. It is 35 degrees Celsius and the sun is shining bright, so they slow down their pace to adjust to the heath. There are only very few tourists here, and Ken and Julie are able to complete their tour around the compound in less than an hour. They continue their drive for 25 kilometers to Ayutthaya, which is a UNESCO World Heritage site. This was the former capital, which is now a ruined old city. The city was founded in 1350 AD and around the 1600s it had a population of already one million and was one of the richest and most cosmopolitan cities in Asia with 2,000 golden temples. Most of the city was destroyed over the ages in several wars with Burma and only some ruins remain, however. The ruins cover a large area, and the driver has to make two stops for sightseeing. There are a lot more tourists at this location than at the previous stop. Finally they visit a temple which has one of the largest bronze Buddha, 12 meters high and as well as two beautiful Jade statutes.

By mid afternoon they are back at the hotel, and enjoy their early dinner of salmon and veggies at the fitness bar. Early evening Ken and Julie explore the shopping area close to the hotel and they walk around the main street and through shopping malls and the elevated pathway for almost one hour and a half. They pass several shrines of which one is famous for the four-faced Buddha, where a group of Thai traditional dancers entertains the tourists. The dancers keep repeating the same movements with hands, arms and legs during one minute, while a live band plays the traditional Thai dance music, where tourists take pictures and videos while seated in front of the dancing ladies. It is slowly turning dark and Ken's shirt is drenched with sweat. Along the walkway back to he hotel, they pass small food stalls, offering cheap meals. You can buy a plate of food for only 50 Baht ($1.40). Many sell fruits, noodles and rice dishes, satay, and sweets; however, Ken doesn't try them for concerns of hygiene.

Bang Pa-In

Jade Buddha Statues

Ayutthaya

Buddha Face in Tree

Vimanmek Mansion and Throne Hall

The next day Ken has a relaxed morning reading his spiritual books. Early afternoon he and Julie take a taxi to the Dusit Park in the city, where they arrive in 40 minutes at the Vimanmek Mansion. After the rain and thunderstorm of last night, the temperature is much milder and enjoyable. The entrance fee is already paid for, as it was included in the ticket price for the Grand Palace, which Ken visited several days ago. This mansion is said to be the world's largest golden-teak building; it has 72 rooms and was constructed without a single nail. Inside it exhibits the furniture and decorations at the time the royal family used to live there, which is from 1901. At this mansion visitors are not allowed to take pictures, nor wear shoes. The shoes need to be stored in the basement of the building, where it smells enormously of sweaty feet/shoes from the many tour groups. One of the service people working in that area is walking around with a Vicks inhaler stick permanently stuck in one of his nostrils. When Ken wants to enter the mansion, the security tells him that it isn't allowed to carry a camera. There is a possibility to store bags and equipment in a locker, but that is in a different building, and Ken doesn't feel like walking all the way back there. So after some discussion, they decide that Ken makes the tour alone, leaving Julie with the camera waiting outside. They agreed that in case the tour is worthwhile, Julie would make it by herself upon Ken's return. Ken moves quickly through the hallways and rooms, pushing passed the many tour groups blocking the route. At the end, Julie doesn't go inside anymore, as there was nothing special to see; there were mostly furnished rooms from the last century. The next building they visit requires a 10-

minute walk through the park. It is the Throne Hall, which was constructed in 1903 as an accompanying Throne Hall for the Vimanmek Mansion. The Throne Hall is now used as showroom/museum for traditional Thai arts and crafts, and exhibits golden thrones, beautiful carpets, jewelry, porcelain, etc. Many of the articles displayed are stunning. Also here, taking pictures is not allowed, but shoes do not need to be taken off. Women need to wear a dress; trousers are not allowed for them. The entrance ticket needs a separate access stamp, which must be obtained in a separate building. Like at the Mansion, there are large crowds of mostly Chinese tourist groups blocking the way outside the building, queuing at the entrance, and in the corridors throughout the Throne Hall building. Ken stores his camera in a locker and for 50 Baht ($1.45) Julie buys a sarong to cover her legs. After their viewing they get their camera and bag from the locker, and Julie sells the sarong to another tourist for 40 Baht ($1.15).

Vimanmek Mansion

Dusit Park

Throne Hall

Royalty Billboards

Marble Temple

The couple is happy to walk away from the crowds, and with the help of the street map, Ken quickly finds the way to another sightseeing object, the so-called Marble Temple, Wat Benjamabophit. It is the most recently built temple in central Bangkok, originating from 1911. The walls of the main temple building are made from Italian marble, and this building has a crucifix shape and stained glass windows depicting Thai mythological scenes. For 100 Baht ($2.85) Ken buys two tickets enabling them to access the compound and enter the main temple building. Inside the main temple, it is not allowed to wear shoes, which need to be left outside the entrance doors. Quite unusual, however, it is allowed to take pictures. As it is already late afternoon, there are only a few tourists. Like at every tourist attraction, also outside this temple there are several metered taxis and tuk-tuks waiting to transport the tourists. It is Ken's experience that whenever he gets a taxi at the hotel, the driver always uses the meter. But when he takes a taxi from the street/city back to the hotel, the drivers always want to haggle and never use the meter. This time Ken agrees on 250 Baht ($7.10) because of evening traffic. It is the typical Bangkok evening traffic: almost nothing moves, tuk-tuks scoot in front of the cars from all sides, scooters and motorcycles move in between the queues of cars to the front of the traffic lights. Several hundred meters before the hotel they leave the taxi because it is stuck in traffic without moving an inch. In the hotel room Ken finds seven red roses in a vase. That is so thoughtful of guest relations, since they are aware that they are staying for such a long time at their hotel.

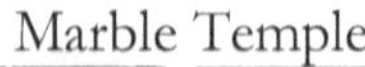
Marble Temple

Phloen Chit Road

Today is all about shopping malls. After their usual waking-up time and breakfast, Ken and Julie go out to explore the several malls along the Phloen Chit Road. They take the Skytrain for two stations, from Phloen Chit to Siam station, which costs only 22 Baht ($0.63) per person for a 10-minute ride. The Skytrain is a new, clean and air-conditioned metro line running at an elevated level above the streets of Bangkok. It is ideal to avoid the busy, congested and overheated streets. In total there are three lines crossing through Bangkok. At Siam station they enter the Siam Center mall directly via the skybridge. It is a mall without the big brand names, but with tasty and reasonably priced restaurants. The best indication that these restaurants are reasonably priced is that Ken sees many students in school uniform eat there. The couple walks around and checks some restaurant menus, after which they cross the square to the Siam Paragon mall. This is the high-end brand mall and one of the largest in Bangkok. They browse through several stores and floors. At a bookstore he buys a compact Thai-English language/phrasebook. By 2 p.m. they are back at Siam Center mall to eat at a Korean/Japanese restaurant. After lunch the couple uses the skywalk to get to the Gaysorn and Central World malls, and later continue to the Central Chidlom mall and via a connecting bridge to the Central Embassy mall. The air-conditioning at the malls is set at a cold temperature and they need long sleeves and long pants, or even a sweater or cardigan, to maintain a comfortable body temperature. When walking outside from one mall to another, Ken's limbs slowly defrost, until after 10 minutes the heat overtakes the cold of his inner core. By the time Ken gets out of the Central Embassy mall, the high-end mall closest to their hotel, it is already dark. Having had a full and late lunch, they skip dinner. The last hours of the day Ken spends in the hotel room, blogging and watching a movie on Cinemax TV.

Skytrain

Siam Paragon mall

Bangkok Traffic

Floating market

After a restless night, because of the loud music coming from the entertainment area outside the hotel, the alarm wakes Ken up at 6 a.m. Ken and Julie have an early breakfast and shortly after seven in the morning depart with a taxi. Yesterday, Ken pre-arranged a taxi to take them on a full day of sightseeing to the floating market as well as the River Kwai Bridge, which are both West of Bangkok. It is the same taxi driver who took them from the airport to the hotel. He has a minivan taxi, which is more comfortable in the back seat, where you can adjust the back of the seat and arm rests. The taxi drives them for almost two hours before getting to a spot where longtail boats depart to the floating market. The local lady selling tickets wants 2,000 Baht ($57) per person for a one and a half hours longtail boat trip. That is too much compared to what the taxi driver charges them for a whole day (3,000 Baht ($86)), so Ken negotiates her price down to 1,000 Baht ($28) per person. They have a longtail boat just for themselves. A longtail boat is a low boat with a non-covered truck engine at the back, and it is really loud and smelly of exhaust fumes. The propeller is at the end of a long shaft, with which the captain also steers, by simply lifting the shaft with propeller out of the water and putting it in the water at different angles from the boat. Their captain wants to stop at many small souvenir shops along the canals, but Ken waves him to go past. Only at one shop Julie buys two gifts. The floating market itself is interesting, but it seems to be more like a tourist attraction. The Thai locals sell fresh fruits, coconuts, and also warm food, having small barbecues and cooking woks on their narrow barges. The canal is congested with tourists in longtail boats. Having toured through the narrow canals, the captain speeds back to the pick up point, where Ken and Julie disembark and drive on with their taxi.

Floating Market

River Kwai Bridge

It is an almost two hours drive (because there is no highway) to Kanchanaburi, the location of the famous River Kwai Bridge. The first stop in town is to visit the war cemetery. It holds the graves of 6,982 allied soldiers representing less than half of the 16,000 soldiers that lost their lives building the railway. The second stop is the large parking lot close to the river Kwai Bridge. From there they walk towards the river, while the taxi driver stays at his car at the parking lot. He indicates that in case Ken looks for him, he will be at one of the small restaurants around the parking lot. He will wait for them till they are done sightseeing. At the riverbank Ken quickly finds a restaurant with view on the bridge. The couple has lunch outside in the shade of a parasol, but it is still hot, 37 degrees Celsius caused by a bright sun in a cloudless sky. They like the food: spicy papaya salad, shrimps with asparagus, omelet and fresh coconut water. For only 500 Baht ($15) per person it is a great deal with a great view. From there they have a short walk to the famous bridge. They join the many tourists that walk across the railway bridge. Prisoners of war and Asian laborers built the bridge during 1942/1943 under the watch of the occupying Japanese army. Little of the bridge is still original, as allied forces bombed most of it in 1945. The laborers had to build a 400 kilometers railway track, linking Thailand to Burma. When Ken gets back home, he will need to watch the movie with the same name from 1957, starring Alec Guinness. At one of the many souvenir shops, Ken buys pants with Thai elephant print, to wear at home as house pants. They quickly find the taxi in the parking area. The driver was already waiting in the car and had put sunshield on all windows to fend off the bright sunrays. Still, the interior is hot and it takes a while before the air-conditioning overturns the heat and changes the temperature in the car to a comfortable level. The drive back to Bangkok is more than 130 kilometers and takes three hours to complete. Particularly the last 15 kilometers in Bangkok take almost an hour. It was a long day with 11 hours on the road, so Ken is asleep early and quickly.

River Kwai War Cemetery

River Kwai Bridge

River Kwai

Railway Bridge

Progress Towards Objectives

How did Ken progress towards his objectives during the 25 days in Bangkok?

The time in Bangkok was great for him to alleviate the work stress of the past 30 years and to escape the cold weather at home. During the first week he did most of the sightseeing and basically saw all the famous sights in and around Bangkok. During the second and third week Ken mostly spent time at the hotel, at the poolside, in the gym, or in the shopping malls in close range. The weather was really warm, between 33 and 38 degrees Celsius, depending on whether there were clouds or not. Coming out of the chill of the air-conditioned malls, restaurants and hotel, it often felt like a warm blanket. Ken really enjoyed the hotel, as they had a large guest room, and enjoyed good breakfasts and dinners. The hotel offered excellent sports classes and fitness equipment, and was in a good location for reaching the malls. Ken was often behind his MacBook for administration and emailing. He did not suntan; he left that for when he is at Thailand's beaches in the next two months. Further entertainment consisted of going to the cinema on the fifth floor of the Siam Paragon mall, where there is a large Cinema multiplex. He saw two movies there. Before the start of the movie, they played the two-minute long national anthem while showing a video promoting the King, during which everybody stood. As it turns out, the Thai people are very patriotic towards their King and Queen. There are many billboards of them on the streets, posters in the malls, and portraits in the hotels. The cinema was extremely cold, even though Ken came prepared with long sleeves and long pants; he was still cold and glad to walk out into the warmth when walking back to the hotel. He and Julie also visited the Karaoke area near the Cinema complex at the Paragon mall. Singing for an hour, taking turns and doing some duets was a lot of fun, despite Ken's bad singing.

They often took the Skytrain to the Siam City mall, and had their lunch at the Korean BBQ. They grilled their own food, chicken, beef, salmon and okra. This cost only 800 Baht ($23) for two people. Healthy and tasty food contributes to feeling good.

The main objective for the three months stay in Thailand was to do something good for the body and mind, but also to give and make a lasting positive impact on some of the people that Ken would meet.

Ken had a heavy focus on sports: cardio, body-toning classes, yoga classes, weights, stretching. He regularly had two or even three hours of sport per day. Combining this with a low carb, high protein diet, without alcohol, sweets and deserts, he felt good physically. Especially the yoga was really good for his body, as it induced stretching and focus on breathing. The latter contributed to peace of mind as well. Another thing he did for his body was giving it sufficient sleep. Although he needed time to adjust to the time difference, generally he slept well and definitely a lot longer than when still working.

Ken visited all the interesting sites, temples, palaces, and historical areas in and around Bangkok. He was very impressed with many of them. Most of these sites were Buddhist religious temples and he saw beautiful Buddha statues and temple decorations. It was however not as spiritual as in Tibet; there he could see monks practicing Buddhism, with the smells of incense and butter candles, chanting, prayers, offerings and more mystiques of the old buildings and small dark chambers. The places Ken visited in Bangkok were mostly swamped with locals and tourists, full of light and missing monks. Although beautiful to see, from his viewpoint several spiritual aspects were missing. Still it contributed to his spiritual mind. A special contribution in this sense was the super friendliness and always smiling Thai people. Those people that Ken got to know better, like Chati, Hathai, the other gym instructors, the waiters and waitresses at the breakfast restaurant, but also the concierge, have shown him genuine kindness and compassion through smiles, warm greetings and kind words. It had a powerful and contagious influence on him.

For the development of his mind, Ken read several books titled: 'An astronauts guide to life on Earth', 'How geographical Maps evolved over time', 'Travelling to work (Michael Palin)', 'What makes you not a Buddhist', 'The art of happiness', 'In his own words'. The latter two books are from the Dalai Lama. Ken made three page-book summaries of the 'An astronauts guide to life on Earth' and 'What makes you not a Buddhist' to capture their essence. Ken and Julie had lengthy discussions about the books on Buddhism, and their views on these concepts. Ken wrote a lot, not only the book summaries, but also essays on the topic 'why are we on earth, what is the purpose of life'. The Michael Palin book he gave away to the business center at the hotel. The Astronaut book he gave to Hathai. Ken said that the books on Buddhism made him think about life's concepts. He was beginning to see events in his life from different perspective.

Ken also fulfilled the third objective of making a lasting positive impact of the lives of others. Hathai is 25 years, studies at Bangkok University to become a diplomat, and finances her studies by working as waitress at the JW Marriott Bangkok hotel. She comes from a poor family in the province, northeast of Thailand, close to the Cambodian border. Recently, she had to take the 13-hour bus trip to go home and help out with the rice harvest during three days. It was only her mother, sister and herself doing the harvesting. As she said, she had to get up at 4 a.m. and worked till dark on the rice paddies, all manual labor. Despite these circumstances, she is positive and friendly and always smiling. This is a perfect example of how happiness is not determined by external factors, but mostly by a person's internal state of mind. Ken gave her the book 'An Astronauts Guide to Life on Earth' from Chris Hadfield. He did this for two reasons. First, the book had some really good tips about achieving seemingly impossible goals. That can help her achieving her diplomat's goal, and not give up along the way. It also contained some good advice how to work in teams. Ken had a copy of his three page book summary printed at a nearby print shop, and stapled this to the inside of the book. Second, it was a large enough book, with hard cover, to enable him to glue a hand written note on A-4 Marriott letter paper to the inside of the front cover. In this letter he commented on her nice personality and not to give up on her dream of achieving a job as diplomat. He also included an envelope with money, to provide a little support for financing her studies, which was probably the equivalent to several months of gross salary for her. The next day she told Ken and Julie that she cried when reading their message. She wrote to Ken in email: "Thank you so much for everything. Your special gift is a part of my study, my house and my life. I will never forget about you."

Points to Contemplate and Personalize

Think about the following questions. Do this thinking in silence and without distractions. Take out a sheet of paper. Write down your thoughts as detailed as possible. Put the sheet of paper away for at least one night. Before you go to sleep, clear your mind and only contemplate these questions in your mind and ask your subconscious mind to provide guidance. Immediately after waking up the next morning, contemplate these questions and answers again. Do this in silence and without distractions. Take your sheet of paper and make any required adaptations to the answers. Ideally you should not go about this alone, so discuss the results with your life's partner or another person whom you deeply trust and rely on. Your life's partner may be able to give you an outside perspective and stimulate critical thinking. Link your answers to the results of the previous step. Make sure that they are consistent and the results of this step build upon the results of the previous step. Repeat this process till you are satisfied with the results.

Key questions:

What is your baggage from the past that you keep carrying around?
What change do you need to empty your baggage?
What reading material will be able to help you on your way?
Are you open to fill your baggage with new content, such as experiences, reflections and outlooks?

Keep in mind:

Your life happens in the now, neither in the past nor in the future.

Your progress:

Your contemplation and personalization of these topics round off step two from the Seven Simple Steps. You have now created awareness that you have an existing situation that needs to be addressed. You understand the concept of the purpose of your life and why it matters that you fulfill the purpose of your life. You have opened your mind and you are letting go of old baggage. You have taken up reading of books, which help you obtain new perspectives. Take your time in this step two, as emptying your teacup needs adequate self-reflection. Slowly start filling your mind with new knowledge and perspectives.

Step 3

Ko Samui: Reading and Taking Inventory

On Tuesday 1 December 2015 Ken wakes up early at 6 a.m., long before the alarm. The couple has breakfast and says their goodbyes and utters their gratitude to the staff at the restaurant. The lady at the juice bar knows exactly which juice Julie wants, and the cook at the egg counter only needs to see Ken to start preparing his omelet. Fruits get brought to their table, without having to ask for it. They know Ken drinks a cappuccino, and he doesn't need to ask for it anymore. Back in their room, Ken does some administrative work behind the computer while Julie reads on the couch in the sun. After being done, Ken shaves his head and showers. He packs their suitcases and by 11 a.m. they walk out of the hotel to a close by money exchanger to change $2,000 in Baht, as it is a place with a really good exchange rate. It is very hot outside and Ken soon starts sweating, as he is already dressed in long pants and shirt for the flight later that day. Back at the hotel he takes a bit of time to cool-off. They say goodbye to the waitresses and the sports instructors and by noon they are checked out and in a taxi to the airport.

40 minutes later the couple arrives at Suvarnabhumi airport and pay the driver 500 Baht ($14). They are quickly checked-in at the Thai counter for flight TG287 to Ko Samui. Their bags weigh 25 and 24 kilograms, but the check-in hostess makes no fuss about it. As it is a domestic flight, security queues are short and they quickly find the Thai lounge and spend the next two hours there. After waiting another hour at gate B5, the flight takes off on time at 3:40 p.m. The plane is quite large, but almost empty. An hour later it touches down on the runway of the small island of Ko Samui. The airport is small and cute, like in Bhutan. There is only one small luggage belt and their suitcases are one of the first to come out. They walk out of the

arrivals to find a taxi, and book themselves on a shuttle-van that brings them together with five other couples and their luggage to their hotels. After two stops and a 25-minute drive, Ken and Julie get to their hotel and pay the driver 340 Baht ($9.70).

Flight TG287

Samui Airport

Renaissance Ko Samui Resort

Ken checks into the Renaissance Ko Samui Resort and Spa on day 27 of their journey. At the front desk they are extremely friendly and upon entry they ask them if they want to use mosquito repellant. Because Ken wears long pants, he declines, thinking that it would not be necessary. But during the check-in process Ken is indeed bitten in three places at his bare ankles. So it seems that there are many mosquitos here, which is quite the opposite of Bangkok where Ken was not troubled by these little vampires. The General Manager of the resort comes to greet Ken and Julie, so does the Restaurant Manager and the Chef. They feel very warmly welcomed and being made part of the local family of the hotel. The front desk lady shows them to their room, which is convenient and small, but not the luxury they had in Bangkok. The resort is separated in two areas: the main area comprising the lobby, restaurants, cultivated gardens, Spa, garden villas and beach side pool are directly situated near the beach, whereas a long building with the normal guest rooms and a garden view swimming pool are at the other side of a street. Ken and Julie have their room on the third floor (out of four floors) in the long building that is connected via a sky-bridge over the street to the main lobby building. Behind their building there is a patch of uncultivated land, not belonging to the resort, where jungle plants grow freely.

The next morning Ken is sticky from the warmth and humidity. They slept without the air-conditioning, so that they could hear the sounds of nature, the nocturnal animals (frogs croaking) and in the morning (birds chirping), which was a relief from Bangkok's busy streets and nightlife loud music. They find the breakfast room easily, across the street towards the beach. Breakfast is fine, but small compared to the JW Marriott Bangkok. The view from the breakfast restaurant towards the sea is beautiful, however. It is hot and humid, and it feels similar to Bangkok, despite being close to the sea and green hills in the islands interior. A thunderstorm approaches and it rains for the next hour. Ken spends time on the balcony of their room. It is really lovely and relaxing on the balcony, under the fan, and with an outside Jacuzzi. Ken spends the afternoon reading and watching a video about extreme pilgrimage on YouTube.

Late afternoon Ken and Julie walk out of the resort to check out the surroundings. He quickly finds a supermarket on the main road, where they buy mosquito repellent and drinks. They continue their walk along the main road towards the center of town and pass many 7-Eleven's, and a local market until they arrive at a large Tesco's. Who would have thought that this small island would have such a Hypermarket? They buy muesli, Greek yoghurt and other food to enjoy in the hotel room. It is dark (after 6 p.m.) when they exit the Hypermarket, and take a taxi back to the resort. Ken needs to negotiate with the driver, and agrees on 200 Baht ($5.70) for two and a half kilometers, seven-minute ride.

As in Bangkok, the Chinese tourist groups are the majority of the guests at the resort, as well as on the sightseeing locations. Though here on the island the groups were much smaller, mostly families or couples or small groups fitting in a minivan, instead of large coaches. Their influence is also noticeable on the menus at the resort's restaurant. For example for breakfast, the restaurant offers full warm Chinese meals, with two or three variations. Most vacationers at the resort seem to stay relatively short, particularly the Chinese tourists, just one or two nights. Ken and Julie seem to be long-term visitors with their 20 days. They see many other tourists come and go during their period of stay.

Renaissance Ko Samui Resort

Weather

Balcony

Street around the island

Local market

Dad's Day

Saturday fifth of December is a special day for the Thai people, as it is dad's day, the celebration of the Kings 88th birthday, who has been in hospital for a long time already. The local newspapers as well as the TV show commemorate celebrations to honor the King. Housekeeping leaves a leaflet in the room that they will light candles and sing some songs early evening for the same purpose. The weather on Ko Samui doesn't cooperate with the celebrations, as it rains the whole day, heavy rainfall in the morning, lighter rain in the afternoon, and only early evening it dries up. The temperature is nice at 25 degrees Celsius. Ken spends the day on the balcony, working on his MacBook to set up his own website, while listening to Christmas songs playing from his iTunes.

Mosquitos

By 4:45 a.m. Ken wakes up from the heavy rainfall, and takes a while to fall back asleep. By 7:30 a.m. he slowly wakes up and sees that it is sunny. They have their breakfast on the balcony where Ken is immediately bitten by mosquitos. It feels very warm on the balcony because of the high humidity, though it is only 32 degrees Celsius. A bit later they move to the beach to enjoy the cooler breeze. Ken settles under some trees, out of the sun, but soon bird poop and other tree related things start falling on him. And of course Ken is bitten several times by mosquitos. So he moves under a roof and puts on mosquito repellent. Still Ken is bitten several times. By 11 a.m. he gives up and moves back to the balcony. He switches on the ceiling fan, lowers the blinds, lights the mosquito candle on the floor, and dives in his book. Still Ken is bitten several times. For lunch they checkout the resort's four restaurants and their menus. As it is too hot to sit outside in the sun, they have their meal inside the Banana Leaf restaurant. Within two minutes at a table near the window, Ken has two mosquito bites on his ankles. The waiter comes with repellent, but it is already too late. Ken enjoys the salad with fresh coconut water. They spend the rest of the day and evening on their balcony. Ken uses the MacBook to write and continues to work on the website, while Christmas oldie sounds come from the Internet radio. Later that night Ken hears a thunderstorm and heavy rain.

Hin Ta and Hin Yai

On a day that the weather cleared and the rain clouds subsided, Ken and Julie spend a good five hours, about 10 kilometers, walking from their hotel to the beaches in the West. They need to walk along the busy road until they have beach access. The goal of their walk is the Hin Ta & Hin Yai rock formations. The Hin Ta is called the grandfather rock, Hin Yai is the grandmother rock, and are local sightseeing rock formations, as they resemble the male and female genitalia. The beach walk was nice; after all, it was their first beach walk after having been in Thailand for 35 days. On their way back they make a stop for a late lunch at McDonalds, of which there are two on this small island. On the way back to the hotel they visit Tesco's and Makro Hypermarkets to buy some food. Ken is happy that they had a mostly overcast day, so that it wasn't so warm, but on the walk back to the hotel it starts raining again. The next day they have a short walk towards the East, to Leam Nan beach. It is warm and sunny, making the beach and shallow sea look beautiful.

Resort beach

Lamai Beach

Sunset

Inland forests

Hin Ta

Lamai beaches

Local street Leam Nan beach

Around the Island

For this occasion Ken hires a car. A little Suzuki Sport to take them around the island, to visit the various beaches and sights. It costs only 1,000 Baht ($30) for the day. The car is beaten, dented and rusty with paint coming off the roof, and its stick shift doesn't really want to cooperate without force, but that is all okay, as these trades make the little car look rough. By 10 a.m. they leave the hotel at Lamai beach, and start a clockwise tour around the island. Since Ken has already been in Thailand for five weeks, he is used to the traffic on the left and has no difficulty driving on the left side, though using the manual gear with the left hand takes a bit of practice. First he fills up the tank for only 800 Baht ($23), after which he drives to the two main Namuang waterfalls on the island. Before getting to Namuang waterfall nr. 2, there is a safari park with monkey shows, tiger pictures, elephant rides, Jeep safari, etc. They skip the safari park and hike up the steep hill.

Although it is mostly overcast, sweat pours from the pores on Ken's back. They first walk on a concrete road, which the safari jeeps use to bring the paying guests to the waterfall; subsequently they take a left turn and hike up a narrow jungle trail, across large boulders and dense forest. Having arrived at the foot of the waterfall, the view is disappointing. The left half of the waterfall is dry, and at the right half only a weak flow comes down the mountainous landscape. They consider hiking to the top of the waterfall, but decide against it, as they don't expect anything better there. They walk back to the car, and drive to the Namuang waterfall nr. 1, which is a lot smaller, more cultivated for tourists and thus less interesting. Their little Suzuki takes them down the mountain again, onwards to Thong Tanote Beach, on the South side of the island, where many small fishing boats lay anchored along the beach. Ken drives along the West side of the island and passes Nikki beach and onwards to Nathon, the main city with a car terminal pier for ferries to other islands. Ken finds the North side of the island not so interesting, at least, until he arrives at Fisherman Village at Bo Phut, and after that the Big Buddha and Wat Plai Luam. They make a stop at these attractions to take pictures and enjoy the local scenery. The temples and statues at these last two locations are large and beautifully decorated, shaped and colored and very worthwhile seeing. There are only a handful of tourists at these locations. The drive back to Lamai Beach is via the East side of the island. The East side has long stretches of hotels, resorts, bars, and is highly commercial. Shortly before arriving at the hotel it starts to rain, while most of the day was dry with overcast or sunny weather. The drive around the island was less than 50 kilometers. Most towns, hotels and resorts are along the coastline and along the main double lane road. The inland is mostly jungle, forests and coconut and banana plantations. Its highest point is 635 meters above sea level, with only few roads to the center of the island. Ken's conclusion of their trip around the island: The South beaches are the most beautiful, particularly at Lamai. Their own resort beach is behind a reef causing a shallow sea and only small waves. But there are probably more nice secluded beaches behind the walls of the many hotels.

Namuang Waterfall nr. 2 Thong Tanote Beach

Fisherman Village

At Big Buddha

Wat Plai Luam

Angthong National Marine Park

During one of their last days on Ko Samui, Ken and Julie planned a day trip to the Angthong National Marine Park. This Marine Park covers 42 small islands close to Ko Samui. As it is a package trip organized by a local tour operator, they get picked up at 7:30 a.m. by a minivan. On its way to Nathon town, the minivan picks up three more couples at other hotels. The group arrives at the boat pier and after paying 600 Baht ($17) Marine Park admission fees they can embark the boat. There are about 50 people on board, and it takes one and a half hours westward to reach the first island. The sea is calm, and the sun cuts through the light clouds. Ken sits on the upper deck under a roof cover, enjoying the fresh and cool sea breeze and the wide views, while Ko Samui disappears in the distance and the islands of the National Park come closer. The boat lets them off onto a longtail boat, which brings them to the island where they make a short, but steep, hike up a hill. Up there, there is a beautiful view on the emerald green lagoon, an island internal lake. Because of lack of wind and the exercise of the climb, Ken is soon covered in sweat. The view on the sea and other islands is spectacular. Back at the beach, many other tourist boats arrived, and the small beach is crowded with tourists. The next activity is sea kayaking. Ken sits at the back of the kayak while Julie sits at the front and does all the pedaling. Ken holds the camera and takes pictures of the amazing rock formations causing other kayak tourists around them to laugh, as they see Julie do all the hard work, while Ken relaxes behind her. The route takes them along the limestone cliffs of the island, through narrow schisms and below overhanging cliffs to another beach. Julie paddles for about 45 minutes to reach that other beach. From there the group is picked up by a longtail boat and brought back to the large boat, where a buffet lunch is offered. The food is basic and simple, but not much to Ken or Julie's taste, so they don't eat much. During lunch the boat moves to another island. Again the group disembarks on a longtail boat, which transports them to a beach. The island offers a hiking trail with panoramic views, snorkeling and sun bathing. Ken and Julie decide for the hiking trail, but after 50 meters it seems like the whole trail is covered with sharp coral rocks, is very steep and narrowly winds through the tropical jungle. As they are only wearing flip-flops, and not sturdy hiking shoes, they decide to let it be. It would be too dangerous to complete that trail without proper shoes. As the couple doesn't want to go snorkeling or sun bathing, they sit down at a restaurant and walk along the small beach. It is very nice there, the white sand and the secluded beach surrounded by green tropical hills. After one and a half hours the longtail boat transports them back to the big boat, which takes them to Nathon in yet another 90 minutes. They disembark at the pier and quickly find their minivan that drives them back to the hotel at Lamai beach, after dropping off the other couples. By 6 p.m. they are back in their room.

Get on board

Angthong National Marine Park

Emerald lake

Sea Kayaking

Angthong National Marine Park

Progress Towards Objectives

How did Ken progress towards his objectives during the 20 days on Ko Samui?

The best example that he was able to alleviate the work stress of the past 30 years, was that he didn't need the alarm anymore to wake up in the mornings. He generally woke up between 7 and 8 a.m., depending on the time he went to sleep the night before. Ken hadn't worn his watch in several weeks. This was a really good sign; it showed that his inner-clock found its new routine, and that he was no longer a slave of time. He had freed himself.

For his body he had a balanced program as well. He had only two meals per day. Breakfast generally consisted of fruits, muesli and yoghurt. The second meal was usually around 3 p.m., comprising of low carb/high protein food, like fish, vegetables, satay or gado-gado. For lunch the couple regularly visited the Swiss restaurant 'Röstiland' on the same street as their hotel. They offered good Thai food for a reasonable price. Ken lived without alcohol, and drank a lot of mint/green tea. He definitely felt a cleansing of his body. Compared to Bangkok, his sports activities were very limited. The gym at the resort was very small, with only limited equipment, so Ken only went a few times. He missed the yoga and fitness group activities from the hotel in Bangkok.

Ken definitely escaped the cold weather from home. On Ko Samui, it was generally between 25 and 32 degrees Celsius, depending on whether it was overcast or sunny. Especially after the rain, it cooled down to a nice temperature. The island was very green, and there was usually some sea breeze providing cooling. It was a lot better than in Bangkok, where the heat stayed trapped between the buildings, in the concrete and asphalt, under overpasses, and where the cars and air-conditionings generated additional heat. In Bangkok it had hardly rained during his stay. Here there was a lot of rain and according to the locals, the monsoon should have ended by the end of November; still it rained a lot into December. There were many days where it was overcast and rained most of the day.

Apart from the few days of sightseeing trips and walks, Ken spent most days at the resort. His stay at the resort was driven by three main factors: there was really not that much to do on the island, many of the days were cloudy and rainy, and he wanted to progress with reading, writing and setting up his own website. During those days he would retreat to his balcony, and keep busy there. Julie would light the Baygon anti-mosquito candle, incense, and play Christmas music from the Internet radio. He spiritually developed his mind by reading a lot and watching relevant videos on YouTube. He read 'the art of happiness' from Dalai Lama; 'Sapiens, A brief history of humankind' from Yuval Noah Harari; their Thailand travel book; and some books on writing. He streamed movies and watched documentaries and interviews such as with Neil Degrasse Tyson - Astrophysics, and Peter Jones - Extreme Pilgrimage. Thinking about life, his life was greatly stimulated by these books and videos.

Still his thought processes had not yet come to a conclusion what it all meant for himself. Will he reach a conclusion during his stay in Thailand, or would that need more time? Linked to that question was the question of the next steps after the three months in Thailand. Bangkok and Ko Samui had been great for reading, writing and letting go of the past. Will Ko Phuket contribute to finding the purpose of his life?

Points to Contemplate and Personalize

Think about the following questions. Do this thinking in silence and without distractions. Take out a sheet of paper. Write down your thoughts as detailed as possible. Put the sheet of paper away for at least one night. Before you go to sleep, clear your mind and only contemplate these questions in your mind and ask your subconscious mind to provide guidance. Immediately after waking up the next morning, contemplate these questions and answers again. Do this in silence and without distractions. Take your sheet of paper and make any required adaptations to the answers. Ideally you should not go about this alone, so discuss the results with your life's partner or another person whom you deeply trust and rely on. Your life's partner may be able to give you an outside perspective and stimulate critical thinking. Link your answers to the results of the previous step(s). Make sure that they are consistent and the results of this step build upon the results of the previous step(s). Repeat this process till you are satisfied with the results.

Key questions:
What is your contribution to society?
Can you increase your contribution?
Can you be more efficient and effective in your contribution by linking it to your passion?
Can you reach other people and improve their lives by following your passion?

Keep in mind:
When you follow your passion, all contributions will feel effortless.

Your progress:
Your contemplation and personalization of these topics round off step three from the Seven Simple Steps. You have now created awareness that you have an existing situation that needs to be addressed. You understand the concept of the purpose of your life and why it matters that you fulfill the purpose of your life. You have opened your mind and you are letting go of old baggage. You have taken up reading of books, which help you obtain new perspectives. Take your time in this step two, as emptying your teacup needs adequate self-reflection. Slowly start filling your mind with new knowledge and perspectives. You have taken inventory of your contribution to the life of other people. You have linked this to your passion. This was mostly thinking work for you, which you did in silence.

Step 4

Ko Phuket: Relaxing, Reading and Thinking Culminating in Vision

On Sunday 20 December 2015, day 46 of his overwintering, Ken wakes up at 5:15 a.m. They had already packed last night, so after fresh up, they are quickly done packing the last items like the toiletries. They enjoy breakfast shortly after 6 a.m., and are back at the lobby half an hour later. Ken and Julie said their warm goodbyes to the waiters/waitresses. As he had already settled the bill the night before, they can leave with the pre-arranged taxi on time. It takes them only 20 minutes to get to the airport. At this early hour there is little traffic. The airport is small, and they are checked in quickly. There are no queues at security, or at check in. They walk over to the gate, via an outside lane, and wait for half an hour. The plane is just a small turbo propeller, with 80 seats. Only 11 of these seats are occupied. There seems to be little activity at the small airport this early, and only few people fly from Ko Samui to Ko Phuket. The ferry would have been another, slower alternative. The flight is only 40 minutes and lands as early as 8:15 a.m. at Phuket International Airport. The bus brings them to the domestic terminal, where they quickly find their luggage (at one of only two luggage belts). Before exiting the arrivals, Ken buys a taxi ticket to the hotel for 600 Baht ($17). They have fixed prices, no bargaining. During their stay on Ko Phuket they find out that the taxi business seems to be in the hands of only a few companies, who keep competition low. The taxis generally don't have or use meters, but instead have fixed, high, prices depending on the location where you want go. Many of the taxis Ken used were minivans, instead of the regular sedan taxis as he had experienced in Bangkok. Even the tuk-tuks on Ko Phuket weren't the small three-wheelers like in Bangkok, but small open minivans. As it turns out, it is only a 20-minute drive to the hotel, which is North of the Airport. After the taxi leaves the main street, it seems like they drive to the middle of nowhere; there are only green bushed fields and a lake and some other resorts along the street parallel to the beach at Mai Khao.

Renaissance Phuket Resort

The lobby of the Renaissance Phuket Resort & Spa is nice and open, with a Christmas tree in the middle. Check-in is easy; though Ken has a bit of discussion on the location of the room. The front desk manager gives them a temporary room 208, as the other room (320) will only be available after 4 p.m. By 10 a.m. they settle into the temporary room and a few hours later Ken and Julie go to the beach grill called 'Sandbox' for lunch. Late afternoon a porter helps them move their bags to the other room. They unpack, change into swimwear, and tour the facilities, pool and beach. The resort has 26 Garden Villas, and two four-story buildings with about 180 guest rooms in total. There are lush gardens and patches of white sand (instead of grass) at the center of the compound. The main restaurant is away from the beach next to a pond where small fish fight for the breadcrumbs thrown in the water by the guests. From here it is too far away and behind the garden to see the Andaman Sea. However, from the large and long infinity pool it is only 50 meters across a green garden to the beach. It is so much larger and nicer (but also higher price category) than the Renaissance Resort on Ko Samui. It seems new and was probably rebuilt after the 2004 Tsunami. The rooms are designed with light colors and high quality materials. Ken can foresee that he will really enjoy himself for the 28 days that he will be here. The couple makes a romantic beach walk while the sun sets.

Ken quickly finds his new daily routine at the Renaissance in Ko Phuket. He generally wakes up between 7 and 8 a.m. (no alarm needed), has his breakfast, and before 10 a.m. Ken and Julie head out to the beach for a long walk on the sandy beaches either to the North or South of their resort. The daily two-hour beach walks are a good exercise for the calves and legs. Ken tries to walk directly along the waterline where the sand is hard, but depending on the waves, he often needs to walk through either soggy or very loose sand, in which his feet sink ankle deep. He walks barefoot, which causes the sand and small seashells to act as a peeling, so after each walk the soles of his feet are sensitive. But all that is compensated by the sunny weather, fresh breeze from the Andaman Sea, seawater cooling his feet, the nice views and romance of the situation. Upon their return by noon he spends another one to two hours tanning, or under the parasol at the poolside, relaxing from the walk and continuing the reading or writing. They go back to their room to shower, wash away all the sand, and get ready for a late lunch. They usually take lunch at the Sandbox restaurant, close to the pool, having a club sandwich, Caesar salad, pizza, burger or fajitas with fresh coconut drink. By late afternoon he is usually back in the room to update the blogs, writes his essays, emails, reads interesting online articles about astrophysics, etc. At around 6 p.m. the couple visits the beach again to watch the sunset, which is very romantic with deep colors of orange and red. Every other day, Ken does a short workout in the small gym. Early evening they stream a movie or watch TV and are generally asleep before 10 p.m., tired from the walk and sunshine.

During the four weeks at the Renaissance Resort Ken sees many other couples and families come and go. The Russian tourists seem to form the largest group, not only at their resort, but also along the other parts of the beaches, shopping malls, as well as restaurants. The Chinese tourists seem to be the second largest group, followed by Europeans.

Resort Lobby

Guest rooms

Pool area

Mai Khao Beach

Ken and Julie are at Hat Mai Khao beach, the longest stretch of beach on Phuket, at over 17 kilometers of golden sand, with a coarse underfoot of the many splintered seashells. The waters are very clean. The beach is part of the Sirinat National Park, as a result of which developments are low key and there are no jet skis, banana boats and other tourist attractions along the beaches. That can all be found at Patong beach. The tour guidebook says that sea turtles come ashore to lay their eggs between November and February. During the many daytime beach walks they never saw any, however. The hotel staff informs them that the sea turtles hardly come there anymore because of the tourism, and that they have migrated to the more desolate Northern beaches. The resort is at around 2/3rds North at Hat Mai Khao beach, and during their walks they cover the whole 17 kilometers. It is about six kilometers to the North-end, and about 11 kilometers to the South-end. Towards the South-end, the beach is adjacent to the starting/landing strip of Phuket International Airport. That means that planes fly in very low when approaching the beach. And when they take off, their jet stream blasts the sand off the beach (the only runway is from West to East). Some tourists intentionally stand in the jet stream. Several times during the moon cycle, and particularly at full moon, the waves at Mai Khao beach are ferocious and reach a three-meters height when they are only 10 meters away from the shore. As there are strong currents during those times, the resort displays warning flags to caution the guests for swimming.

Mai Khao beach

3 meter waves

Landing strip

Sunsets

Immigration Office

Ken and Julie arranged for a 60-day tourist visa before arriving in Thailand. As that visa is due to expire at the beginning of January, they visit the

Immigration Office in Phuket town at the end of December. Ken arranged for the resort shuttle to bring them to Phuket Town and back. After breakfast, the shuttle bus takes almost an hour (including a stop at the nearby JW Marriott resort) to get them to a small mall in Phuket Town. The road to get there is busy, with the usual small stores, shops, workshops and restaurants on the side. After they get out of the mini-bus, a tuk-tuk driver approaches them. He offers to take them around town for only 200 Baht ($5.70), until they have to depart again at 4 p.m. with the resort's minivan. Ken accepts the offer as it is a good price, and asks him to drive them to the immigration office. It takes about 10 minutes, while they see that the town is small, with no apparent points of interest. There are many tourists at the immigration office and Ken needs to queue to get the TM-7 form. He fills it out and needs to make copies of his passport/visa pages and a pass-photo. But then it is 12:00 noon, and everybody gets sent out of the office; it is the officials' lunch break. They will be open again for business at 1 p.m. As there is nothing to do around the immigration office, Ken and Julie take the tuk-tuk to a nearby mall, where they spend the next hour killing time. Ken is back at the immigration office by 1:10 p.m., and the long queues have already formed. He has his photo taken (in a small office next door), registers the forms, and waits till his number is up. In the end he has a 90-minute waiting time, while the actual processing time by the civil servants is about 10 minutes. He needs to pay 1,900 Baht ($53) per person, which is relatively expensive. The tuk-tuk driver brings them back to the initial mall where they have a late Japanese lunch. The sushi, salad, tempura and mochi ice cream taste excellent. They are back at the resort by 5:30 p.m. His conclusion for the day: a visit to Phuket town is not worthwhile, along the way there was nothing of interest to see, and immigration officials need their time (several were reading the paper and watching TV while only one worked).

Patong Beach

Early January Ken and Julie make a day trip to Patong Beach. Ken has pre-arranged the resort shuttle, which departs from the lobby early afternoon. The resort shuttle is a cost-efficient alternative to the expensive taxis. It takes the minivan one and a half hours to get to Patong beach, because of the 65 kilometers distance, and the traffic jam getting into Patong town.

The beach there is crowded with parasols and sun chairs, like the mass beach tourism on Mallorca or Miami. You can rent jet-skis and banana-boat or parasail behind a speedboat. The stretch of beach is only three kilometers long. It is late afternoon by the time they walk out of the restaurant where they had a Japanese lunch. They browse through a mall, shops and a department store, which have a number of popular brands, though not the real high-end. They slowly make their way back to the main street along the beach. Along the way Ken books their speedboat trip to James Bond Island at one of the many small tour operator desks. He obtains a price which is 50% lower compared to the rates the travel desk at the resort or in the nearby mall offer. They see many souvenir shops selling hats, t-shirts, bikinis, flip flops, and fake LV, YSL and many other bag brands, as well as fake Rolex and other watches. For a LV man's weekend bag they only ask 2,500 Baht ($70) and for the real looking LV scarf only 900 Baht ($25), before any negotiations. Of course Ken leaves it; he doesn't want to support the counterfeit products industry. Along the walkways there are long line-ups of alternating stores: souvenir shops, sightseeing travel shops, massage parlors, tattoo shops, restaurants and tailors. At each of these shops, the local sellers call out and try to get the tourists in their establishment. Like in Bangkok, also the sewage in Patong causes a nasty odor along these shopping lanes. Bright neon flashes on the buildings, and loud music coming from all directions, including some tuk-tuks, which have serious sound systems installed. As much was destroyed by the Tsunami of 26th December 2004, the buildings, including hotels and malls, look new. Patong Beach Road, Thanon Bangla, is very crowded and alive with one bar screaming loud music after another, alternated by tattoo-shops, massage parlors, 7-Elevens and an occasional fast food chain like McDonalds. Lady-boys parade on the street, and men and women flash leaflets to lure you to 'ping-pong' shows. Together with several other hotel guests, they share the minivan back to the resort, and little after midnight they are back in their room, happy to be able to shower-off the sweat, dust and smells.

Patong

Tiger Kingdom and Central Festival Mall

Two main tourist attractions on Ko Phuket are the Tiger Kingdom and the Central Festival Mall. After breakfast Ken and Julie take the hotel shuttle bus to the Central Festival mall. It departs at 10:15 a.m., drives to Phuket town to let off other guests, and then continues to the Central Festival mall. One and a half hours later they arrive. Ken immediately searches for another taxi to take them to the Tiger Kingdom. One takes them in a 10-minute ride for 200 Baht ($5.70). Ken asks the taxi driver to wait for them at the Tiger Kingdom and drive them back to the mall after they are done. At the Tiger Kingdom they select the Tiger sizes (large, medium, small or smallest) to have pictures taken with. Ken selects the large tiger for a 10-minute photo op and pays the 800 Baht ($23). There are a lot of tourists, and he needs to wait 45 minutes till it is his turn. Ken enters a large outdoor cage where three large tigers reside, where the caretaker guides him how to proceed with the large cats. As others are not allowed in the cage, the caretaker takes the pictures of Ken with the tigers. The small cubs and large tigers are very lazy, even asleep, as it is around midday, the time they have their siesta. Being in the cage with the large tigers is scary, but the tigers are too lazy to lift a paw. Ken did have to sign a waiver when he bought the tickets; in case you lose a finger or hand, there is a small insurance cover. Upon arrival at the Central Festival mall Ken gives the taxi driver an extra tip, as he had to wait for them at the Tiger Kingdom. After briefly checking out the stores at the mall, they have lunch at an 'all you can eat' sushi and shabu-shabu place. This menu costs only 375 Baht ($11) per person, including soft drinks and ice cream. It is very cheap, but quality is disappointing (he should have expected that for such a low price). After lunch they roam through the mall, and find a bookstore with an English section where he can finally stock up on new books. Early evening they find a taxi to bring them to Phuket Town Limelight mall, from where the hotel shuttle picks them up shortly after 9 p.m. An hour later they are back at the resort, eager to shower and rinse off the Tiger smell.

Tiger Kingdom

ATV and Elephant Rides

The tourist guides for Phuket all write about exciting experiences of ATV and elephant rides, and Ken and Julie do not want to miss out on those experiences. A taxi takes them to an area South of Phuket town, Chalong in an hour and a half. The last kilometers are steep uphill and the views on the bays and inland are very nice. The minibus finally stops at some small wooden houses, where ATVs are parked and elephants are waiting in a coral. After some confusion about the tour package, Ken pays the local owner for a short ATV and elephant ride experience. They mount the ATV and follow the guide for about 10 minutes on the road further uphill. The road ends at the Big Buddha, and the guide tells them that he will wait till they have done their sightseeing there. So they walk further up, take pictures, and buy souvenirs. Ken buys several little wooden hand-painted elephants, which proceeds go towards the maintenance of the Big Buddha statute. Julie needs to wear a sarong to cover her legs; Ken can go in the area with shorts. The large statue is 45 meters high, and was officially completed in 2011, but with still some construction going on at its base. Subsequently they follow the guide on the ATV and slowly drive back to the station. Ken complains to the guide that it is so boring driving on the concrete road. The guide takes the hint, and he guides them on an off-road site for 15 minutes. That is way more fun, but as Ken is the last one, he has to cope with all the dust of the two ATVs in front of him. The 30 minutes off road fun is sufficient; he is glad he did not select a package that includes a 4-hour ATV tour. Back at the station, two large elephants are waiting for them to be mounted at the elephant scaffolding. Ken sits alone on one of them and towards the end of the trip, he is able to sit on the neck of the elephant, like a caretaker. The elephant's skin is rough, leathery, and smelly and the black hairs on the head are sturdy and tickle. The elephants walk slowly and regularly stop to eat from branches along the dust road. After some 45 minutes they return to the scaffolding and are let off. The two caretakers want to sell them some hand-made jewelry, the proceeds of which will go towards the care of the elephants. Some of the jewelry seems to contain ivory. Ken asks them about it, and they state that it is either plastic or baby elephant tooth, but nevertheless, he declines, as he surely doesn't want to buy any ivory. The caretakers complain about the large quantities of food the elephants need, so Ken decides to give them a 1,000 Baht ($28) donation for the care of the elephants instead. There is also a baby elephant in the coral; it is so cute and Ken buys a food basket to feed it. The caretaker makes the little elephant kiss Julie on the cheek (the trunk sucks at her cheek like a vacuum cleaner and makes a soft trumpet-like sound). Back in the taxi, they ask the driver to make a stop at the Central Festival mall, which is close by. He agrees to wait for them for 300 Baht ($8.50). The couple has a Japanese lunch at Fuji restaurant and late afternoon they are back at the hotel. They change into their swimming suits, and wash off the ATV dust and elephant smell in the Andaman Sea and subsequently in the pool. They lie on a sun chair enjoying the warm late afternoon sunrays.

Big Buddha ATV

Panorama Elephant Ride

James Bond Island

Mid January, Ken and Julie undertake a pre-arranged trip by speedboat to the famous James Bond Island. This is another one of the main tourist attractions in the region. The taxi picks them up at 9 a.m. and takes them to the Ao Por Marina Pier, where all tourists are collected and registered. They need to wait about 30 minutes before they can follow the guide to the speedboat. There are a total of 30 people on the boat, so it is rather cramped. The 30-minute speedboat ride takes them via Panak Island to Ko Khao Phing Kan, better known as James Bond Island, famous after the filming of "The Man with the Golden Gun" movie with Roger Moore in 1974. The main attraction here is the Ko Tapu, the 20-meter high limestone cliff in the middle of a small bay. The small island is bustling with tourist groups, while the longtail boats and speedboats wait 100 meters away, as the pier is very small. The beautiful views on the limestone cliffs make up for the crowded environment. The tour guide gives the group 30 minutes to take pictures and browse along the souvenir shops. Subsequently, the speedboat takes the group to Hong Island, where they all disembark on a floating platform. Each couple gets on a sea kayak with a private paddler, who makes a 30-minute tour through a cave, along the limestone cliffs and partially around the island. The waters are choppy, but their kayak stays dry. Back on the platform they have to wait till the whole group is back again, before going on board of the speedboat, which takes them all the to Ko Panyee the so called 'sea gypsy' village. Muslim Indonesian fishermen built the village on stilts. The local population consists of around 350 families, and they have their own Mosque, school, etc. Many tourist boats moor there for lunch so that during the day, the population size increases several times. Ken and Julie have a pre-set lunch of rice, fried mixed vegetables, soup, chicken and omelet, which tastes okay. After lunch they walk around and check out some souvenir shops. The village is on concrete stilts built against a small island, so everything they have in the village needs to be brought over from the main land, including drinking water. At around 2:30 p.m. their speedboat leaves the village and takes them to Naka Island. All guests disembark at the beach for a stay of one and a half hours. Locals wanting to sell drinks, massages or Jet-ski rides immediately approach Ken. He decides to make a 20-minute Jet-ski tour around the Naka Island and negotiates a price of 1,200 Baht ($34). He puts on the life jacket and speeds off. It is nice and fun as the waves are low and high speed can be achieved on the coastal shallow waters. Having done a full circle, Ken swims in the warm seawater and sits down on a sun chair. The sand on the beach is white and soft as flour, much nicer than at Mai Khao, where the sand is yellow and rough because of the shells. By 4 p.m. they have to board the boat and they arrive back at the Ao Por Pier only 10 minutes later. This was a wonderful day seeing beautiful natural sights, doing different activities and enjoying the sun and sea breeze from the speed of the boat.

Speedboat to James Bond Island

Sea Kayaking

Sea Gypsy Village

Naka Island

Naka Island

Progress Towards Objectives

How did Ken progress towards his objectives during the 28 days on Ko Phuket?

At this location, work stress of the past 30 years was alleviated through the long beach walks and the sightseeing trips. Particularly the beach walks gave him time to think, contemplate and debate with Julie about many topics. He addressed topics of their family life, topics of their spiritual developments, what the future would look like, etc.

Ken definitely escaped the cold weather at home. On Ko Phuket, it was generally between 28 and 32 degrees Celsius with a much lower humidity than on Ko Samui or in Bangkok. There was always a sea breeze providing some cooling. Out of the 28 days, there were only a few nights during which it rained and thundered, and only twice during daytime there were short periods of rainfall. What Ken remembered most about the weather were the long sunny days and beautiful sunsets, touching the Andaman Sea in the West. This was in contrast to Ko Samui, where he did not have a view of the sunset because of the position of the resort. Ken did not suntan in Bangkok or Ko Samui, but completely caught up with that at the resort in Phuket.

He continued a balanced program for his body. As on Ko Samui, food intake was limited to two times a day, for breakfast and late lunch and he drank no alcohol. Compared to Bangkok, his sports activities were limited. Of course the-several-hours-long beach walks added to his level of fitness.

The website had matured, so that his attention was mostly on creating content in the form of the daily blogs and essay about the pathway to happiness. He spiritually developed his mind by reading a lot and watching relevant videos on YouTube, as already described before. On 25th December 2015, Christmas day, while sitting at the breakfast table, Ken uttered: "*the purpose of my life is to be a successful Author*". He was surprised himself that this statement suddenly came out. Had he really concluded his thought processes on the purpose of his life? During the past one and a half months he had done a lot of reading of spiritual and self-help books, and had done a lot of writing for his website. As a result of which these activities strongly influenced his subconscious mind, which worked on finding the answer to his question over that time period. Ken had asked himself that question on the first day upon arrival in Thailand, and had made his stay a quest for finding that answer. But he was surprised that it had already come so quickly, only halfway through his overwintering stay. So during the days and weeks after that Christmas day, he thought about it hard and had long discussions with his life's partner. The long beach walks were ideal to contemplate this decision and its consequences, and let it really sink in. Many detailed questions were still left unanswered but the overall vision for the remainder of his life seemed to have been identified. The question of the next steps after the three months was pushed forward, to a future decision. First the vision needed further exploration. Since that Christmas day, Ken felt a wave of relief and excitement at the same time. Can he use the last three weeks of their three months overwintering in Thailand to deepen his vision?

Points to Contemplate and Personalize

Think about the following questions. Do this thinking in silence and without distractions. Take out a sheet of paper. Write down your thoughts as detailed as possible. Put the sheet of paper away for at least one night. Before you go to sleep, clear your mind and only contemplate these questions in your mind and ask your subconscious mind to provide guidance. Immediately after waking up the next morning, contemplate these questions and answers again. Do this in silence and without distractions. Take your sheet of paper and make any required adaptations to the answers. Ideally you should not go about this alone, so discuss the results with your life's partner or another person whom you deeply trust and rely on. Your life's partner may be able to give you an outside perspective and stimulate critical thinking. Link your answers to the results of the previous step(s). Make sure that they are consistent and the results of this step build upon the results of the previous step(s). Repeat this process till you are satisfied with the results.

Key questions:

Do you have a setting conducive to generating your vision?
Does your vision harmonize with the signals from your body, your mind and your spirituality?
Can you derive your vision from what you are already doing by changing perspectives?
Can your life's companion help you as a sounding board to validate the direction of your vision?

Keep in mind:

You should define and follow your own dream, not the dream of another person.

Your progress:

Your contemplation and personalization of these topics round off step four from the Seven Simple Steps. You have now created awareness that you have an existing situation that needs to be addressed. You understand the concept of the purpose of your life and why it matters that you fulfill the purpose of your life. You have opened your mind and you are letting go of old baggage. You have taken up reading of books, which help you obtain new perspectives. Take your time in this step two, as emptying your teacup needs adequate self-reflection. Slowly start filling your mind with new knowledge and perspectives. You have taken inventory of your contribution to the life of other people. You have linked this to your passion. This was mostly thinking work for you, which you did in silence. You have generated the vision for your future. Your vision feels good and you are exited about it. You are slowly realizing that you might have had a breakthrough.

Step 5

Ko Phi Phi: Meditation to deepen the Vision

On Sunday 17 January 2016, day 74 of his stay in Thailand, Ken wakes up before the alarm of 8 a.m., gets dressed and has breakfast at the Renaissance Resort's main restaurant. Breakfast there is good, with a wide variety of food, almost similar to their hotel in Bangkok, and better than on Ko Samui. He and Julie say goodbye to the waitresses, with kind words and tips for their good cares, and they do the same at the Sandbox. In the room they pack the last bits and ask the concierge to collect their two large bags, while Ken checks out and settles the final bill. After the heavy rain of last night, it is still overcast and very humid. In 40 minutes the taxi drives them to the Ao Por Grand Marina on the East coast of the island. At the marina representatives from the resort on Phi Phi Island collect them, register them for the resort's speedboat transfer and take their large suitcases. Ken and Julie follow a group of about 20 other tourists to the boat that departs shortly before noon. It takes more than one and a half hours to get to the Phi Phi Island Village Beach Resort.

Resort speedboat

Andaman Sea

Phi Phi Island Village Beach Resort

In the bay in front of the resort the group is transferred to a smaller boat, as the speedboat can't get close enough to the beach to let them disembark. The smaller boat, by means of a ladder, lets them disembark directly on the beach in front of the resort. This is such a fantastic and special experience. The group is guided to the check-in lobby, which is close to the beach and has no walls, only a roof supported by beams. After 20 minutes Ken and Julie have their room key and a golf cart transports them and their luggage to their bungalow. It is a freestanding bungalow on stilts. The couple only unpacks the limited clothing and toiletries that they need and leave the rest in their suitcases, since they are only staying there for five nights. After so many days on the road already, they have gotten accustomed to using only a small part of their wardrobe. On this beautiful island they expect to wear only shorts, t-shirts and swim wear anyway. In the mean time they came to the conclusion that they packed way too much. In the warm climate of Thailand, combined with two months of stay at its tropical beaches, they are in need of just a limited selection of attire. They are hungry and explore the resort for restaurants. After checking the opening times and menus of several restaurants they end up eating at the bar of the main pool. Ken and Julie order satay, salad and club sandwich to share, as the portions are small and they are hungry. Satisfied and with a full stomach they make a tour around the resort. It is broad along the sea line, but also extends into the hills with lush tropical greens. It is still overcast and not so hot, though very humid and thus sticky. They linger at the activity center to check out what activities they offer. They are extremely impressed with the resort; its location, design, and facilities. Paradise is the right word. In the early evening they take a shower and subsequently settle on the bed. Ken writes the blog, and they discuss their plans for the next days and go to sleep relatively early, as Ken wants to get up early tomorrow morning to start the practice of meditation.

Phi Phi Island Village Beach Resort

TSUNAMI
EVACUATION
ROUTE
320
m.

Meditation

The next day they wake up at 5 a.m. After some emailing and fresh up, Ken heads outside, where it is still dark. He uses a small flashlight to light the way across the sandy pathway down to the beach, where he finds an open empty massage hut to meditate. By 6 a.m. he is in lotus position. This is Ken's first attempt at meditation and it is proving to be rather difficult to hold the lotus position and keep the focus of his mind. Ken keeps it up for an hour with regular interference of having to change positions, leg stretching, finding back support and refocusing the mind, instead of looking around at what the pool cleaners are doing. He never thought it would be that difficult. But after an hour his mind feels relaxed, but the body is sore. How do Monks do this a whole day? He will need a lot more practice, but he is up for the challenge. They have their breakfast at the Marlin restaurant, which has only beams that support a roof, so that the view of the beach and sea are wonderful. There is no sewage smell here, unless the gardeners are watering the gardens. The food itself is good and staff is friendly and helpful.

Meditation at Sunrise

Ton Sai Village

For today the couple decides to hike across the island. The island has no roads, and there are no cars. The resorts and hotels are along the coast only; in the interior there is only jungle and limestone rock formations. Transportation is basically by boat along the shorelines. After a 15-minute hike to the West they arrive at a first beach. Some local people live there and provide longtail boat services. It is low tide and although the bay is very nice, it is not spectacular. They hike an inland-jungle-trail to visit two viewpoints in the interior, high on the hills (186 meters above sea level). The first viewpoint is rather disappointing, as there is not much to see, only the Andaman Sea. The second viewpoint on the other hand is more spectacular, and therefore has quite a number of tourists. The locals use this opportunity to charge the tourists 30 Baht ($0.85) per person to access this viewpoint. There is a magnificent view on a narrow isthmus, which connects two elongated islands. Most tourist activities are concentrated on the main land in between the two bays. To the South is Ao Ton Sai, where all the boats dock to the pier, whereas to the North is Ao Lo Dalam, with a lovely curve of white sand and clear shallow water. There is quite some construction going on, on either side of the isthmus, going up the hills. After lingering at the viewpoint, Ken heads down to the two bays, down a concrete path and many stairs (no more jungle trail). At the foot of the hill, the crowds of tourists increase significantly, together with a compact area of many tourist shops, restaurants, tattoo shops, massage parlors and tour operator desks. Also in Ton Sai Village there are no cars, and the tourists' heavy luggage as well as the supplies for the hotels and stores, are moved through the narrow streets on handcarts, wheelbarrows or on shoulders when it goes up the steps. The small area is bustling with life; vendors calling tourists into their shops, tourists eating in open settings in restaurants, young backpackers looking for a cheap room to stay. And cheap it is indeed: 100 Baht ($2.85) for a simple meal, 800 Baht ($23) for a room with fan and a room with air-conditioning costs 1,800 Baht ($52) per night, disregarding quality. At the pier ferries, tourist speedboats and longtail boats moor to bring many day-tourists and backpackers. The North beach in contrast is wide and shallow and partially surrounded by limestone cliffs. This is the center of all the tourist activities such as sun bathing and sea kayaking. Ken walks around the beach and the bustling streets and visits several souvenir shops. He drinks fresh coconut for only 40 Baht ($1.15). After some time, they head out again and look for the other trail back to their resort, which is supposed to be a shorter coastal trail, away from the two viewpoints. They start walking along the coast but somehow soon end up walking uphill. They do not find out whether they are on the right path, as there are neither signs to guide them, nor do they have a map. After 30 minutes huffing and puffing uphill in the heat of the afternoon, they end up at the second viewpoint. So they definitely took the wrong path. They hike back the same route and by 3 p.m. they are back at their resort, after a 6-hour hike. They are so happy to shower off the sweat, dust and nature (insects, spider cobs). Early dinner is at the Marlin restaurant and they spend the evening in their bungalow watching the movie 'The Beach' starring Leonardo DiCaprio.

Hiking Trail

First viewpoint

Second viewpoint

Ton Sai Village

Ao Lo Dalam

More Meditation

The next days are relaxed and have a similar pattern. Ken wakes up early at 5:30 a.m. because he wants to meditate at the beach while the sun rises. In the dark he walks to the same massage hut. All bungalows are still dark, only the resort's breakfast crew is busy with the preparations for the breakfast, which starts at 6:30 a.m. By 6 a.m. Ken is in lotus position and recites his mantras in his mind. He hears the waves slowly coming towards him, while the tide is coming in, the stiff breeze rustle the long leaves of the majestic palm trees around him, the sound the wind makes while blowing past the shells of his ears, some birds waking up and starting to greet the day, chirping their best song. He smells the salt in the air that is carried with the wind from the breaking wave crests. He feels the humidity on his skin, his joints of his crossed legs ache while in the lotus position, his bottom and feet resting on the hard wood, his fingers touching each other, his belly go in and out with the rhythm of his breathing. He hears his breathing ever so lightly through his nostrils. He is living in the moment during his meditation sessions. After several days of practice, Ken is satisfied with the progress of concentration and holding the lotus position. For an hour Ken controls his mind and steers his consciousness through the repetition of his mantras, in order to embed them in his sub-consciousness. Ken feels at peace with his Self and the Universe, and feels one with the environment around him.

During one of the nights there was a thunderstorm, and the strong wind remained also in the morning. It whips the waves with small white crests before they break on the beach. Despite the strong wind from the East, the waves are very small compared to the three-meter waves at Mai Khao beach in Puket. Here they are perhaps 30 centimeters. The wind brings fresh air, rustling of the palm leaves and washing of the waves. These are nice background sounds while meditating. But within the hour Ken has three mosquito bites, even though he wears long sleeves and long pants; somehow the little vampires always seem to find a way to get to his blood. At breakfast Ken makes an appearance with the other tourists; dressed in his monk-red pants with elephant prints, monk-yellow long sleeved shirt with a big elephants print on it, pirate's headscarf covering a bald head and a full long curly beard, he must look like a hippie to them, but he doesn't care what others might think of him. Since the resort is situated on the East side of the island, they finally get to enjoy spectacular sunrises. During breakfast they enjoy the scenery of the beach and the bay and the light spectacles of the sun rising in the distance over the sea and the distant islands. They are the first guests at the pool chairs or at the beach chairs. There is no better environment for Ken to spend his time advancing his essay on 'the meaning to life', if it wasn't for the mosquitos. After only half an hour on the sun chair, Ken has three mosquito bites, so he moves to the table at the pool bar, where he gets another three mosquito bites within the hour. Aggravated he goes back to the bungalow to spray insect repellent on his legs. Ken starts reading the book 'Your (re)defining moments - becoming who you were born to be'. Late lunch is at the Marlin restaurant and the evenings are spent in their bungalow, as there is not much other entertainment at the resort.

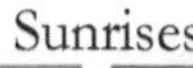
Sunrises

Phi Phi Ley Island

On their last day on the island, the strong winds and choppy waves only subside in the afternoon. So Ken packs a bag for a half-day trip. After lunch they arrange for a longtail boat trip to Phi Phi Ley Island. At 2 p.m. Ken and Julie are back at the small tour office, pay 1,800 Baht ($52), and follow their boat captain Ni to his longtail boat which lays anchored at La Na Bay, a small bay 10 minutes walk on the West side of the island. It is low tide, so they need to wade 50 meters through the low water to get to the longtail boat. Phi Phi Island actually consists of two Islands, the larger one called Phi Phi Don, and the smaller one called Phi Phi Leh, four kilometers South of the larger Island. Their resort is on the inhabited Don Island, whereas Leh Island is a natural park and is uninhabited. At Maya Bay on Leh Island the movie 'The Beach' was filmed in 1998. The island consists mostly of tree-covered high limestone cliffs rising directly from the sea, and has several beautiful bays. Ni takes them along the West coast of Phi Phi Don Island to the South tip, and then crosses the four kilometers to Phi Phi Leh Island to the South. There are still quite some waves, mostly caused by the speedboats passing by. These speedboats come from many other locations, like Phuket, to bring tourists to the famous Maya beach. The waves splash against their boat and spray the salt seawater. The sun it hot but the sea breeze makes it bearable, while they sit under a roof. The captain sails them past the East side of the Leh Island, first past the Viking cave, with sketches drawn by pirates a hundred years ago (so Ken doesn't understand why they call it Viking cave). In the caves there are many birds, whose nests are taken for the preparation of the famous Chinese bird's nest soup. From the sea level, there are bamboo ladders leading up to the caves. Ken signals Ni to keep going; he doesn't want to climb up there. 10 minutes later they come to the entrance of a secluded bay. Because it still low tide, the boat runs aground at the entrance of the Pileh bay. Ni indicates that he can't get any further and pushes the boat free with a long pool. He circles the island to the South and heads up North again to the Maya Bay at the West side. Ni steers the boat slowly into the Bay, where many other longtail boats and speedboats lay anchored. Because it is still low tide, he lays anchor about 50 meters from the beach. Ken and Julie take their bag and step out of the boat into the water, which is knee-deep. Barefoot they wade the 50 meters towards the beach through the clear seawater while avoiding stepping on sharp coral and rocks that cover the seafloor. There are many other tourists in the water and on the beach, and thousands of pictures and selfies are being taken. Ken adds to that number for today. Because is it later in the afternoon, half of the beach is already in the shade. There is a lot of natural beauty, but the tourists also leave their garbage behind, unfortunately showing little respect for this wonderful piece of paradise. Upon arrival Ken needs to pay 400 Baht ($11.50) per person for entering the National Park. After about an hour they wade back to Ni's boat and he slowly backs out of the bay. Ken asks him to sail back to Pileh bay, as by now the tide should be high enough for the longtail boat to get into the secluded bay. He sails past the South point of the island and up North again along the East coast. The water level at the entrance of Pileh bay is indeed high enough for Ni to steer his boat in. He maneuvers through gorgeous gorges with high tree-covered limestone cliffs till the end of the bay. He runs the boat aground at a narrow strip of beach, and Ken gets off to take pictures in the knee-deep water. The water is crystal clear like drinking water with a white sandy ground. After a while Ni sails them out of the secluded bay back to the Andaman Sea, past the North tip of Phi Phi Leh Island to the East coast of the Phi Phi Don Island, and back to La Na Bay. In the mean time the sea has become very smooth. Ken enjoys the view of the tree-covered limestone cliffs and some secluded beaches along the way. Since tide is high Ni docks his longtail boat right at the beach. This was a super romantic and beautiful trip. The views were stunning and locations extraordinary. This three and a half hour longtail boat trip is definitely one of the highlights of their whole stay in Thailand.

On the way to Phi Phi Ley Island

Maya Beach

Pileh Bay

Progress Towards Objectives

How did Ken progress towards his objectives during the five days on Ko Phi Phi?

For his body he continued the balanced program with food intake twice a day and absence of alcohol. Although the resort did have a gym, it was small with limited equipment. Other than the hike across the island, he had shifted his training of the body to the training of the mind, through the daily meditation sessions.

The paradise-like setting of the resort, the sun, the sea breeze, the salt water splashing from the speed of the longtail boats, his slim and tanned body, his smooth and oily skin, all made him remove the work stress of the past 30 years. That past was not on his mind anymore; it was a chapter in his life that was closed. Instead he was now looking to the future.

His attention was mostly on writing the daily blogs and his essay about the pathway to happiness. He continued reading books on the topic of discovering one's true Self. And that is where the present merged with the future. The content of his exclamation on Christmas day was slowly forming. Ken was thinking of possible topics for books he wanted to write, and it made him think about how this came about. During 30 years in corporate environments he had always travelled a lot and he had written many business reports. It was what he loved to do. So what better way than to now do this for himself? His passion had always been travelling and writing, so combining this to fulfill the purpose of his life would be awesome. Can he use his time in Krabi to solidify his passion?

Points to Contemplate and Personalize

Think about the following questions. Do this thinking in silence and without distractions. Take out a sheet of paper. Write down your thoughts as detailed as possible. Put the sheet of paper away for at least one night. Before you go to sleep, clear your mind and only contemplate these questions in your mind and ask your subconscious mind to provide guidance. Immediately after waking up the next morning, contemplate these questions and answers again. Do this in silence and without distractions. Take your sheet of paper and make any required adaptations to the answers. Ideally you should not go about this alone, so discuss the results with your life's partner or another person whom you deeply trust and rely on. Your life's partner may be able to give you an outside perspective and stimulate critical thinking. Link your answers to the results of the previous step(s). Make sure that they are consistent and the results of this step build upon the results of the previous step(s). Repeat this process till you are satisfied with the results.

Key questions:

Do you have enjoyable moments in your pathway?

Does the elaboration of your vision of the purpose of your life lead to feelings of excitement?

Do you take time to recognize and understand your feelings relating to your purpose?

When you turn inward through meditation or other forms, does Your Self strengthen your purpose?

Keep in mind:

You are the wisest person when it comes to knowing who you are and what you are.

Your progress

Your contemplation and personalization of these topics round off step five from the Seven Simple Steps. You have now created awareness that you have an existing situation that needs to be addressed. You understand the concept of the purpose of your life and why it matters that you fulfill the purpose of your life. You have opened your mind and you are letting go of old baggage. You have taken up reading of books, which help you obtain new perspectives. Take your time in this step two, as emptying your teacup needs adequate self-reflection. Slowly start filling your mind with new knowledge and perspectives. You have taken inventory of your contribution to the life of other people. You have linked this to your passion. This was mostly thinking work for you, which you did in silence. You have generated the vision for your future. Your vision feels good and you are exited about it. You are slowly realizing that you might have had a breakthrough. You thought long and hard about your vision. You did this in silence, through meditation. You discussed it with your life's partner and addressed different angles. All results point in the same direction. You are thoroughly enjoying the process and feel excited that you are on the right pathway.

Step 6

Ko Krabi: Laying the Cornerstone for Building the Future

On Friday 22 January 2016, day 79 of their stay in Thailand, Ken and Julie head back to the beach after meditation and breakfast. They enjoy the warmth of the early morning sun on their skin, while at the same time their skin is being caressed by the sea breeze from the East. The sea breeze not only creates waves on the water, but also the golden hairs on Ken's legs and arms dance in the rhythm of the wind. Ken reads his book till 10 a.m., after which he returns to the bungalow to pack. They check out at 11 a.m., but still need to wait till 2 p.m. before the longtail boat sails them to the marine pier at Tomsai Bay. Because of low tide a tractor transports them to the longtail boat. The longtail boat sails south along the East coast of the island, to arrive at the ferry pier. At the Tomsai Bay Pier, Ken buys two tickets for the ferry to Krabi, Ao Nang Beach, for 350 Baht ($10) each. They board the ship, and sail away at 3:30 p.m. Along the way he enjoys the views on limestone islands and cliffs with small white sandy beaches.

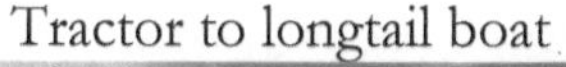

Tractor to longtail boat

Ferry to Krabi

Holiday Inn Resort Krabi

Two hours later the ferry arrives at Ao Nang Beach, which is 42 kilometers North/East from Ko Phi Phi. Because there is no pier, all disembarking tourists are transferred onto longtail boats anchored next to the large ferry. There are 24 people, plus luggage, on a small boat, which tips to one side when the people and their bags are not evenly distributed. The longtail boat sails for five minutes to get them to a small inland bay, and anchors with its front on a small sandy beach, next to many other longtail boats. Ken disembarks at the front of the longtail boat and lands with his feet ankle deep in the water. Suitcases are carried overboard and put on the sand. Ken carries the large suitcases off the beach and hires a tuk-tuk (rather a motorbike with sidecar) for 200 Baht ($5.75) to take them to their hotel. Five minutes later they check in at the Holiday Inn Resort at Krabi, Ao Nang Beach. The resort is more basic (but also at a much lower rate), but has two large pools, sun chairs and pool bars at its central court with a garden around it. The resort is cut-off from the beach by a busy street. After unpacking they cross the street to check out the beach. Though it is dark, it looks nice, flat shallow waters with hardly any waves. Its direction is towards the West, so sunsets should be visible, like on Ko Phuket. Ken visits the hotel's Spa to ask for any meditation areas, but there are none. He concludes that it is probably best to meditate on the balcony of their room on the third floor, facing west. At the hotel's restaurant they have a light dinner before turning back to their room. They shower and Ken writes the blog for the day, does some administration and emailing and falls asleep relatively late.

On one of the days the couple walks out of the resort to the South, along the main street in order to do some shopping. There are hardly any Russian tourists here; most tourists seem to come from Scandinavia, France and Italy. At night they have some excitement in their room caused by a mouse. They have their room on the top third floor with a high and pointy roof. Above the entrance and bathroom there is an elevated space where the air-conditioning unit is installed. It is in this space, about three and a half meters above the floor, where they hear scratching sounds and twice shortly see a mouse on the edge. Ken calls housekeeping, and it takes 30 minutes for a short guy to show up with a short broom and an empty canister of Baygon. As he can't reach the space, even when standing on a chair, he indicates in broken English that he will get a ladder and come back again. Ken waits for 30 minutes and he still does not show up, so he calls the front desk to tell them that they will go back to sleep, and that the housekeeper doesn't need to come anymore.

Arrival in Krabi

Holiday-Inn Resort

Ao Nang beach

Ao Nang Streets

Ao Nang Beach

Most of the five days follow a similar pattern. Ken meditates in the sun chair on the balcony from 6 till 7 a.m., while the sun rises. He could not find a better place for his practice on the hotel premises or the beach. The balcony looks out to the center court of the resort, directly opposite of the restaurant and kitchen. There are many manmade sounds at the time of his meditation, very different from the Phi Phi Island resort. Given the early time, Ken and Julie are usually the first ones to sit down for breakfast at the resort's only restaurant. Staff is friendly, and the cappuccino and other food taste good. The couple explores the beach on this first morning and walk along the Ao Nang beach to the North, about two and a half kilometers, till they come at a river which can't be crossed. At that location all the speedboats and longtail boats lay anchored for the nights and sail off loaded with tourists in the mornings. The beach is flat and the sand greyish, with a lot of shells and seaweed leaving a fishy smell behind. The views towards the limestone cliff formations are again spectacular. In little over an hour they are back at the hotel, having enjoyed the morning sunshine and "fresh air". Ken continues to work on his essay, either on the balcony as long as he has shade, at the poolside under the parasol, or in the room during late afternoon and evening. Late lunch they have at a restaurant three minutes walk down the street or at the resort. At sunset they go down to the beach across the street to admire the red sky.

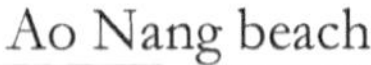

Ao Nang beach

Sunrise Meditation Sunset

Four Islands

For the last day at Krabi Ken booked a half-day longtail boat tour to the 'four islands'. At 8 a.m. they wait in the lobby to be picked up. The tide in front of the hotel is low, and the boat captain called Lau lets them walk to his longtail boat through the shallow water at the bay for a 100 meters. First Lau sails to Tup Island, an exotic tropical island, where at low tide you can walk along the sand bank to the neighboring island. But the tide is high, and it is too dangerous to walk there. Ken needs to pay 400 Baht ($11.50) per person for access to this National Park. Ken compliments the 'beach rangers' for having the most beautiful working place in the world. Upon arrival there were just a handful of people on the small stretch of beach, which has the sea bordering on both sides. Before leaving, speedboats with groups of tourists are disembarking. Ken is happy that he decided for the early morning tour, before the speedboats arrive from many places. The wind causes waves, which in turn spray a lot of water from the bough up onto the boat, as the captain sails them to 'Chicken Island', a rock formation that looks like a chicken. After a picture from the boat, Lau sails on to Poda Island, with high limestone cliffs in its interior, but a beautiful white sandy beach at the South side. Ken and Julie walk barefoot through the soft white sand, till the beach ends in rock formations. After a further 10 minutes sailing the longtail boat arrives at Railey Beach, which is overcrowded with tourists. The couple goes ashore and walks along the beach to the Phra Nang cave, which has a shrine for the sailors to pray for good luck on their journeys. Despite the crowds, the views towards the Andaman Sea and the limestone rock formations are stunning. There are many longtail boats, and even several longtail 'food' boats lay anchored at the nice white sandy beach. As at the floating market outside Bangkok, they sell drinks, fruits, fresh coconut, and they prepare wok-fried and deep fried food on their longtail boats. From there Lau takes them back to Ao Nang beach. It is high tide and they can go ashore directly on the beach now. Ken thanks Lau and gives him a tip. Shortly after 12:00 noon they are back at the resort and glad to shower, removing a thin layer of salt from their skin and sand from their feet. The afternoon is spent having lunch at the resort's restaurant and Julie helping Ken to proof read his essay 'The pathway to Enduring Happiness'.

Getting to the longtail boat

Panorama

Tup Island

Chicken Island

Poda Island

Poda Island

Railey Beach

Phra Nang cave | Food boat

Railey Beach | Back to Ao Nang Beach

Progress Towards Objectives

How did Ken progress towards his objectives during the five days in Krabi?

On all days Ken could enjoy the sunshine, though there were regular clouds as well and a breeze at times. The temperature in daytime was around 34 degrees Celsius, but it felt very humid, much like in Bangkok. Ken missed the fresh sea breeze from Phi Phi Island. He took care of his body through sun tanning, two meals a day and no alcohol. The resort did have a small fitness, but Ken was too consumed by his writing of the essay on happiness, that he did not take time to work out.

His essay on 'The pathway to Enduring Happiness' was his first major piece of writing. So after several long days and late evenings of writing, Ken was relieved that its first edition was finished. In the mean time, Ken had come to the conclusion that his Christmas day exclamation would and could indeed reshape the remainder of his professional career. Through the many books he had read, the long discussions with Julie, the beautiful locations in Thailand and his writing practice of the last weeks and months, he had indeed identified the passion of his life.

The daily meditation at sunrise was slowly changing his spiritual being and mind condition. For two weeks he has been controlling his mind, seeking the silence of the meditation and shaping his spiritual future. Can he let the purpose of his life now take over his life?

Points to Contemplate and Personalize

Think about the following questions. Do this thinking in silence and without distractions. Take out a sheet of paper. Write down your thoughts as detailed as possible. Put the sheet of paper away for at least one night. Before you go to sleep, clear your mind and only contemplate these questions in your mind and ask your subconscious mind to provide guidance. Immediately after waking up the next morning, contemplate these questions and answers again. Do this in silence and without distractions. Take your sheet of paper and make any required adaptations to the answers. Ideally you should not go about this alone, so discuss the results with your life's partner or another person whom you deeply trust and rely on. Your life's partner may be able to give you an outside perspective and stimulate critical thinking. Link your answers to the results of the previous step(s). Make sure that they are consistent and the results of this step build upon the results of the previous step(s). Repeat this process till you are satisfied with the results.

Key questions:
Do you have a cornerstone on which you can build your purpose?
Do you see your focus and energy levels increase?
Do your preparations feel effortless?
Can you identify concrete next steps to realize your vision and purpose?

Keep in mind:
Each journey, however long and whatever the destiny, starts with a single first step.

Your progress:
Your contemplation and personalization of these topics round off step six from the Seven Simple Steps. You have now created awareness that you have an existing situation that needs to be addressed. You understand the concept of the purpose of your life and why it matters that you fulfill the purpose of your life. You have opened your mind and you are letting go of old baggage. You have taken up reading of books, which help you obtain new perspectives. Take your time in this step two, as emptying your teacup needs adequate self-reflection. Slowly start filling your mind with new knowledge and perspectives. You have taken inventory of your contribution to the life of other people. You have linked this to your passion. This was mostly thinking work for you, which you did in silence. You have generated the vision for your future. Your vision feels good and you are exited about it. You are slowly realizing that you might have had a breakthrough. You thought long and

hard about your vision. You did this in silence, through meditation. You discussed it with your life's partner and addressed different angles. All results point in the same direction. You are thoroughly enjoying the process and feel excited that you are on the right pathway. You have put your vision for fulfilling the purpose of your life to the test. You successfully completed the first cornerstone. Your foundation has proven to be solid. You have a clear focus, a clear mind and high energy levels. You feel good doing what you do and it goes effortless.

Step 7

Ko Yao: Living the Purpose of Your Life

On Wednesday 27 January 2016, day 84 of their stay in Thailand, Ken and Julie relocate to Ko Yao, the last location of their three months stay in Thailand. Ken is on the balcony at 6 a.m. for an hour of meditation, followed by breakfast at the resort's restaurant. Before they are being picked up at 9 a.m., he donates two books to the small bookshelves of the resort and checks out. The driver has already arrived and loads their two Rimowa suitcases in the minivan. It takes 30 minutes to drive to the Ao Thalen Pier. The views around the bay are beautiful. Only two other couples embark on the longtail ferryboat together with them. The boat trip takes 40 minutes and passes the Hong Island group, a popular day trip tourist destination for snorkeling and beach hopping. Also here the views on limestone cliff formations and small white sandy beaches are magnificent.

Ao Thalen Bay

Ko Yao Island Resort

At the Ko Yao Pier the captain and his help load off the large suitcases and the tuk-tuk driver organized by the resort is already waiting for them. They drive 10 minutes to the South, and turn into a small road. The first impression of the Ko Yao Island Resort is that it looks small but romantic. Check-in is just submitting their passports. Strangely enough Ken doesn't get a room key. The friendly front desk lady leads them to their room, or rather their sea view villa, which they booked. But as it turns out the view from the villa is on the garden overlooking the back of another villa. So Ken kindly asks if he can change to a sea view villa, because they are celebrating their 25th anniversary this year. The lady walks Ken back to the front desk, where he talks to the reservations lady, who changes their villa to one with sea view. Ken goes over to the new villa and is shown around. Ken and Julie are ecstatic; it is the next level in paradise. Their villa is less than 30 meters away from the beach, with tall palm trees in the front. Though they actually can't see the beach, as their ground level is about two meters higher than the beach/sea level. But they do see the panoramic view on the Andaman Sea and the Pakoh Islands in the distance. Their bed overlooks the garden and sea, has mosquito net, and their room is equipped with sliding doors towards the beach. There is no TV in the villa. At the back they have an open air shower, but an indoor shower in the villa as well. The side porch of the villa has a covered front-open space. It contains lounge chairs, relaxation beds and meditation mats. The thatched roof is directly visible from the inside, and consists of dry palm leaves. The villa even comes with its own allocated sun chair at the beach side, similarly numbered as the bungalow. Although the doors to the room can be locked, they leave them open and only lock away their valuables and notebooks in the room safe. There are only 20 villas in the resort, and Ken and Julie are in Villa nr. 5. Furthermore there is one restaurant, one Spa, one infinity (saline water) pool. The resort is picturesque, cozy and romantic. Ken sits for a while to enjoy the view and contemplates his high level of satisfaction with his three months stay in Thailand. By 3 p.m. they have their late lunch at the restaurant, from where there is the same panoramic view on the Andaman Sea and islands. The Thai food is really good, satisfying their taste buds. The afternoon is mostly cloudy and windy, so Ken sits on the side porch behind his notebook. Before evening falls a lady brings five mosquito candles and places them alongside the inner walls. After darkness has come, Ken and Julie shower under the stars. The mosquito net over the bed keeps them safe from insects, and through the open doors they hear the sounds of the waves.

Ken's five days at the Ko Yao Resort follow more or less the same pattern. He sleeps well the whole night, having found mental peace and tranquility through his mediation as well as having found the purpose of his life, in combination with the sound of the waves, the rustling of the palm trees in the night wind and the fresh air. He meditates an hour on the side porch during sunrise, and after the early breakfast spends the rest of the morning on the sun chair at the pool. There he either reads the book 'The magic of Thinking BIG' by David Schwartz, or he uses the silence to turn inward and think up creative ideas to shape his future. He has his Moleskine exercise book next to him on the sun bed and regularly writes down his thoughts and ideas. Apart from the daily blogs, he does not need to write as his essay was already completed on Krabi. Early afternoon he is back at the villa to use the open air shower in their small back garden and change for lunch. The Thai food during the late lunches tastes fantastic. The remainder of the afternoon he spends on the porch, enjoying the cooling wind from the ceiling fan during the afternoon heat. He regularly steals glances of the beautiful view till it is too dark to see and read. After darkness has settled over the area, the porch light or computer screen attracts too many insects, so he moves inside. The days are usually with clear blue skies and sunny, though on some afternoons a storm would come up with a lot of wind, thunder, clouds and rain. The evenings are cozy under the mosquito net in bed, where he streams a movie. There is no evening entertainment or a gym at the resort, but none is needed.

Ko Yao Island Resort

Sunrises

Hong Islands

On their last day, Ken and Julie join 10 other resort guests for a complimentary longtail boat trip to three of the Hong Islands; about 20 minute eastward sail from their beach. Like the previous small island boat trips they visit picturesque small beaches along high limestone cliffs. Since the group is early, there are not many other tourist boats yet, but these increase in numbers as the morning progresses. Even the unavoidable speedboat loaded with Chinese tourists lays anchor next to them while the group enjoys a small beach. The crew of the longtail boat consists of two sailors, and Pong, the guide, has some nice stories to tell. The boat is shared with two French couples, one Swiss couple with two small girls and an English couple. At the small resort, the majority of the guests speak either French of German. The waves are low, and the wind and speed of the boat sprays the salty water on Ken while seated close to the bow of the boat. This is such a welcome cooling from the heat of the sun. The group is back at their own beach after three hours, and Ken tips the crew. In the shade of their veranda, Ken and Julie talk about the success of their three months in Thailand, how Ken has progressed during that time and what the next three months will look like. They discuss how they will need to find a new daily routine back home and how they will miss the sea, beaches, sun and smiles of the local people.

Hong Islands

Final Departure

On their day of departure, the early morning ritual is the same as before. He and Julie have a last dip in the Andaman Sea and hug each other while in the water. They are 'in the moment' and dream away for a minute, realizing that they are living their dream. They enjoy it knowing that today they need to travel back to the cold in their home country. They shower, pack their bags and check out. Ken pre-arranged all transport to Phuket airport, so he just needs to sit back and enjoy the rides. First they have a 15-minute drive with a tuk-tuk, which takes them to Manoh Pier, on the South side of their Island Ko Yao Noi. There they wait for 30 minutes till the speedboat leaves to take them to Bang Rong Pier on Ko Phuket. They arrive 30 minutes later, and upon disembarking the taxi is already waiting to drive them to Phuket International Airport. They arrive there shortly before 1 p.m. As their flight only leaves at 4:30 p.m., Ken first changes from his shorts and short-sleeved shirt into long sleeved shirt and long pants, after which he checks in their two Rimowa bags. Together they weigh more than 45 kilos and he has them checked through to their final destination. He obtains the boarding cards for the two flights, and sits down at a restaurant for lunch. They linger there for a while until it is time to go through security and immigration, after which they walk around the shops. Boarding and departure are on time. The plane takes off towards the West, so they fly low over the beach where he had stood to observe the planes land several times before. The flight to Bangkok is uneventful and is only an hour and a bit, but it gives Ken time to think and create more ideas for his next steps. At Suvarnabhumi airport they disembark via the stairs, and a bus takes them to the transit terminal. After security check they quickly find the Thai Silk lounge where they wait for the next four hours. Before walking to their gate, they browse through some shops and a bookstore, always on the look for new spiritual material to further develop their minds and knowledge. They board the Thai Airways flight shortly after midnight. In the mean time it is Monday 2 February and it is day 90 of his overwintering. Before falling asleep in the uncomfortable position of his economy seat, his last thought is "*I love my life which is becoming even more beautiful every day*".

Points to Contemplate and Personalize

Think about the following questions. Do this thinking in silence and without distractions. Take out a sheet of paper. Write down your thoughts as detailed as possible. Put the sheet of paper away for at least one night. Before you go to sleep, clear your mind and only contemplate these questions in your mind and ask your subconscious mind to provide guidance. Immediately after waking up the next morning, contemplate these questions and answers again. Do this in silence and without distractions. Take your sheet of paper and make any required adaptations to the answers. Ideally you should not go about this alone, so discuss the results with your life's partner or another person whom you deeply trust and rely on. Your life's partner may be able to give you an outside perspective and stimulate critical thinking. Link your answers to the results of the previous step(s). Make sure that they are consistent and the results of this step build upon the results of the previous step(s). Repeat this process till you are satisfied with the results.

Key questions:

Is the purpose of your life taking over your life?
Are your body, your mind and your spirituality being elevated to the highest level of happiness?
Do you now have concrete plans in place and in execution to realize the purpose of your life?
When comparing to the beginning, do you now feel like being catapulted in a new life because you are moving with the flow instead of trying to swim upstream?

Keep in mind:

Your feelings are your best feedback mechanism.

Your progress:

Your contemplation and personalization of these topics round off step seven from the Seven Simple Steps. You have now created awareness that you have an existing situation that needs to be addressed. You understand the concept of the purpose of your life and why it matters that you fulfill the purpose of your life. You have opened your mind and you are letting go of old baggage. You have taken up reading of books, which help you obtain new perspectives. Take your time in this step two, as emptying your teacup needs adequate self-reflection. Slowly start filling your mind with new knowledge and perspectives. You have taken inventory of your contribution to the life of other people. You have linked this to your passion. This was mostly thinking work for you, which you did in silence. You have generated the vision for your future. Your vision feels good and you are exited about it. You are slowly realizing that you might have had a breakthrough. You thought long and hard about your vision. You did this in silence, through meditation. You discussed it with your life's partner and addressed different angles. All results point in the same direction. You are thoroughly enjoying the process and feel excited that you are on the right pathway. You have put your vision for fulfilling the purpose of your life to the test. You successfully completed the first cornerstone. Your foundation has proven to be solid. You have a clear focus, a clear mind and high energy levels. You feel good doing what you do and it goes effortless. You made concrete plans to fulfill the purpose of your life and identified the next steps. You are geared to action and can't wait to make it all happen. Your teacup is full again. Filled with excitement and anticipation for a future to have a lasting and positive impact on other people's life.

The Travel Guide to Self-Actualization

Finding out the purpose of your life is not an easy thing to do. Some people indeed find their purpose and live their passion, but many struggle in their daily existence and never obtain that exciting feeling of what they are doing is meaningful for them and others.

The Purpose of Ken's Life

What developed during the three months of Ken's overwintering in Thailand was remarkable. For the first time in many years, perhaps for the first time in his life, he had time to think about questions such as who am I, why am I on this earth, what should my contribution to others be, and how can I find enduring enlightenment and happiness. The many books that Ken read during these three months provided him with guidance to find the answers to these questions. The books did not give him the answers, but provided a structured thought process on how to process such questions. Ken is still not done reading, but has come so far in his own thinking and consciousness about the answers, that he feels confident that the answers that he found are the 'right ones' for this stage of his life.

His true Self has found its place in the Universe, the role he is meant to assume in order to generate a lasting positive impact on the lives of others: to be a successful writer. This is fusing having a purpose for others together with living his passions. This gives meaning to his life and helps other people advance on their path to their own purpose of life (whatever that purpose may be).

The Purpose of Your Life

Let some time pass after completing the Seven Simple Steps. Look back how your life took a new turn. Did you have the courage to go through with it? Is the fulfillment of your purpose in life sustainable for you? Are you indeed reaching other people, and are you indeed providing a contribution to the improvement of their life? When the answer to those questions is a firm yes, and you feel excited and exhilarated, keep doing what you are doing, because you are living the purpose of your life.

Two Interwoven Story Lines

As you will have read, this book has two story lines interwoven: the experiences of three months overwintering in Thailand at 6 locations including the most beautiful beaches, combined with the story of finding the purpose of life. How did Ken achieve his objectives during the three months in Thailand? How did he alleviate the work stress of the past 30 years? How did he spiritually develop, think about life to find his passion, and decide the next steps after the three months? How did he give back to society? How did he escape the cold winter weather from home? Each of the six locations played their own role in achieving his objectives. The descriptions of the roles of these six locations gradually showed the developments that Ken went through during the three months in Thailand. The development stages of his thought processes coincided with the changes in locations where each location provided its own contribution.

Bangkok was the first stop and had a strong focus on physical development. The physical development was driven by partaking in many fitness and yoga classes, as well as cardio and weights lifting in the large fitness of his hotel. It was further supported by a conscious diet of two meals per day with high protein and low carbohydrates, combined with complete abstinence from alcohol. Through the heavy focus on these sports, his body and mind started to work off the work stress of the last 30 years. It took time to get used to the time difference and the 30 degrees Celsius temperature difference. During the almost four weeks in Bangkok, reading and writing had a slow start. Bangkok was very central for exploring the Thai cultural heritage through sightseeing trips, which caused a high level of distraction from the working past. Exploring the new sites, smells and sounds and meeting the kind, smiling and warm-hearted people gave a great boost to changing his state of mind. From Buddhism standpoint the stay in Thailand was a bit disappointing: the temples, statues and shrines were very nice, but Ken missed the practicing monks and mystique of the dimly lit chambers, smells of butter candles and incense. Weather-wise it was too hot and humid in between the buildings in Bangkok, which was not so enjoyable.

Ko Samui was the second location. Because of the rainy weather, stinging insects and the limited sightseeing places on the island, Ken spent most of the 20 days on the balcony of his room at the resort. That was ideal to progress with reading and developing his website. Ken was able to give back to society by creating a website and fill it with content to share knowledge and experiences with other people. Filling content meant writing, and that is where the writing of essays about the purpose of life and related subjects developed.

Ko Phuket, though only 40-minute flight from Ko Samui, had a completely different type of weather. Ken started tanning on that location, caring for his body by changing his pale colorless winter complexion into an evenly colored brown complexion. Ken felt good soaking up the sunrays and its vitamin D (of course with the appropriate UV-protection). Ken took up the physical development again, by making long beach walks. Apart from that, the time in Phuket was mostly spent reading, thinking, writing and relaxing. Due to the relaxing and thinking time during the long beach walks, he received the vision of his future life. The 28 days there had done him well. In Phuket much time was spent on the beach and at the pool, where his relaxation level reached the peak of the three months stay in Thailand.

On *Ko Phi Phi* Ken started his meditation in a paradise-like setting. Ken was very relaxed, which gave him the tranquility to sit down for meditation, and he was very focused, believing to have found his passion in becoming a writer. His focus developed the need to find silence and contemplate about how to follow his passion. Such answers did not come automatically and during his meditation sessions he could go deeper into the subject matter. At the same time writing about the pathway to happiness as well as caring for his tanned body continued. The trip on the longtail boat to Phi Phi Ley

Island was probably the best experience of the whole three months, and elevated his happiness to the highest level.

Krabi was the fifth location and had all focus on completing the essay about the pathway to happiness. The content of this essay was the result of reading many spiritual books on the matter at hand, as well as Ken's own thought processes about happiness. It formed the foundation for his future activities, a manuscript that he can use as the foundation for a book. The 10 days of meditation had confirmed his beliefs and choices. Becoming an Author is the purpose of his life. With that, his relaxation level, which was so high while on Ko Phuket, was already subsiding. Ken is a person who has an extremely high drive and turns this drive into energy to achieve his goals. Since his life's goal had become clear, he began working towards that goal. That is why on Krabi all his focus was on completing his essay. It actually coincided with the fact that for him there was not much of interest in or around Krabi.

The last five days of the three months were spent on *Ko Yao*. The quietness and tranquility were definitely a climax in finishing off three months in Thailand. Meditation and the environment were a highlight, inducing reading and thinking. Through his writing practice during the last three months, Ken had indeed identified the passion of his life. Not only had he identified the passion of his life, he was slowly realizing that he was actually already living his passion for writing. The thinking solidified Ken's plans for his future. By that time, he had concrete plans what the next months would look like: writing and publishing his books.

Ken's Future

The future was clear and bright. Ken was physically relaxed, recharged, and had a tanned, slim and fit body. Ken was mentally prepared to follow his passion, and spiritually he was ready to give back to society through his books.

Your Future

Take out your sheets from the Seven Simple Steps. Complete your final sheet by describing your future. Hopefully your words describe your future as clear and exciting as Ken's.

Seven Simple Steps

Think about the following questions. Do this thinking in silence and without distractions. Take out a sheet of paper. Write down your thoughts as detailed as possible. Put the sheet of paper away for at least one night. Before you go to sleep, clear your mind and only contemplate these questions in your mind and ask your subconscious mind to provide guidance. Immediately after waking up the next morning, contemplate these questions and answers again. Do this in silence and without distractions. Take your sheet of paper and make any required adaptations to the answers. Ideally you should not go about this alone, so discuss the results with your life's partner or another person whom you deeply trust and rely on. Your life's partner may be able to give you an outside perspective and stimulate critical thinking. Link your answers to the results of the previous step(s). Make sure that they are consistent and the results of this step build upon the results of the previous step(s). Repeat this process till you are satisfied with the results.

The Seven Simple Steps to a life of meaning for yourself and other people are:

1. Creating awareness that you have an existing situation that needs to be addressed, introducing the concept of the purpose of your life

Key questions:
Do you know what the passion of your life is?
Do you improve the life of other people?
Do you struggle in your daily existence and never have that feeling of excitement that what you are doing is meaningful for yourself and others?
What part of your life would you like to change to give it meaning and passion?

Keep in mind:
Your life is under your full control, and if you don't like certain aspects of your life, it is up to you to initiate the changes.
The answers to these questions usually have a high correlation to the stage of your life, unless you are in a transition from one stage to the next.

2. Letting go of past baggage

Key questions:
What is your baggage from the past that you keep carrying around?
What change do you need to empty your baggage?
What reading material will be able to help you on your way?
Are you open to fill your baggage with new content, such as experiences, reflections and outlooks?

Keep in mind:
Your life happens in the now, neither in the past nor in the future.

3. Read up on your materials and take inventory

Key questions:
Do you have a setting conducive to generating your vision?
Does your vision harmonize with the signals from your body, your mind and your spirituality?
Can you derive your vision from what you are already doing by changing perspectives?
Can your life's companion help you as a sounding board to validate the direction of your vision?

Keep in mind:
You should define and follow your own dream, not the dream of another person.

4. Relax and think to come to your vision

Think about the following questions:
Do you have a setting conducive to generating your vision?
Does your vision harmonize with the signals from your body, your mind and your spirituality?
Can you derive your vision from what you are already doing by changing perspectives?
Can you life's companion help you as a sounding board to validate the direction of your vision?

Keep in mind:
You should define and follow your own dream, not the dream of another person.

5. Expand your vision

<u>*Key questions:*</u>
Do you have enjoyable moments in your pathway?
Does the elaboration of your vision of the purpose of your life lead to feelings of excitement?
Do you take time to recognize and understand your feelings relating to your purpose?
When you turn inward through meditation or other forms, does Your Self strengthen your purpose?

<u>*Keep in mind:*</u>
You are the wisest person when it comes to knowing who you are and what you are.

6. Putting your vision to the test: laying the cornerstone for building the future

<u>*Key questions:*</u>
Do you have a cornerstone on which you can build your purpose?
Do you see your focus and energy levels increase?
Do your preparations feel effortless?
Can you identify concrete next steps to realize your vision and purpose?

<u>*Keep in mind:*</u>
Each journey, however long and whatever the destiny, starts with a single first step.

7. Start living the purpose of your life

<u>*Key questions:*</u>
Is the purpose of your life taking over your life?
Are your body, your mind and your spirituality being elevated to the highest level of happiness?
Do you now have concrete plans in place and in execution to realize the purpose of your life?
When comparing to the beginning, do you now feel like being catapulted in a new life because you are moving with the flow instead of trying to swim upstream?

<u>*Keep in mind:*</u>
Your feelings are your best feedback mechanism.

Your progress

Your contemplation and personalization of these topics round off the Seven Simple Steps.

You have now created awareness that you have an existing situation that needs to be addressed. You understand the concept of the purpose of your life and why it matters that you fulfill the purpose of your life.

You have opened your mind and you are letting go of old baggage. You have taken up reading of books, which help you obtain new perspectives. Take your time in this step two, as emptying your teacup needs adequate self-reflection. Slowly start filling your mind with new knowledge and perspectives.

You have taken inventory of your contribution to the life of other people. You have linked this to your passion. This was mostly thinking work for you, which you did in silence. You have generated the vision for your future. Your vision feels good and you are exited about it. You are slowly realizing that you might have had a breakthrough.

You thought long and hard about your vision. You did this in silence, through meditation. You discussed it with your life's partner and addressed different angles. All results point in the same direction. You are thoroughly enjoying the process and feel excited that you are on the right pathway.

You have put your vision for fulfilling the purpose of your life to the test. You successfully completed the first cornerstone. Your foundation has proven to be solid. You have a clear focus, a clear mind and high energy levels. You feel good doing what you do and it goes effortless.

You made concrete plans to fulfill the purpose of your life and identified the next steps. You are geared to action and can't wait to make it all happen. Your teacup is full again. Filled with excitement and anticipation for a future to have a lasting and positive impact on other people's life.

Recommended Reading

To help you to different perspectives on the pathway to finding the purpose of your life, consider the following reading:

Byrnes, Rhonda. *The secret*, London: Simon & Schuster, 2006.

Canfield, Jack. *Key to living the law of attraction*, Deerfield Beach: Health Communications, 2007

Canfield, Jack. *The success principles: how to get from where you are to where you want to be*, New York: HarperCollins, 2007

Carnegie, Dale. *How to stop worrying and start living*, New York: Simon & Schuster, 1984

Collier, Robert. *The secret of the ages*, New York: Tarcher/Penguin, 2007

Dalai Lama, *In my own words: an introduction to my teachings and philosophy*, New York: Hay House, 2011.

Dalai Lama, *The art of happiness, a handbook for living*, New York: Riverhead Books, 2003

Harari, Yuval Noah. *Sapiens, a brief history of humankind*, London: Vintage, 2011

Hill, Napoleon. *Think and grow rich*, New York: Tarcher/Penguin, 2005

Jones, Dennis Merritt. *Your (re)defining moments–becoming who you were born to be*, New York: Tarcher/Penguin, 2014

Khyentse, Dzongsar Jamyang. *What makes you not a Buddhist*, Boston: Shambhala Publications, 2008

Merton, Thomas. *New seeds of contemplation*, New York: New Directions, 2007

Schwartz, David J. *The magic of thinking big*, New York: Simon & Schuster, 2012

Sharma, Robin. *The monk who sold his Ferrari*, London: Thorsons, 1997

About the Author

drs. Hans Beumer is an enthusiastic and seasoned traveller and a passionate Author. He has travelled all over the world for business and leisure, exploring many different cultures. Since February 2016 he is fulltime Author and Global Traveller.

Throughout his lifetime, Hans Beumer has had an energetic drive to accomplish his goals. His personal vision is to make sure that his own goals generate a high added value contribution to the lives of other people. He sees it as the purpose of his life to help other people advance in their life. Privately he engages in philanthropy and supports the under-privileged children in India to help them advance to a meaningful life through education and a healthy and secure learning environment. As an Author he shares his experiences with the world, in order to give back to society. His books are the carrying vehicles of his passion, and their publishing enables him to reach and touch the lives of many millions of other people on all continents. It is hard work, but this hard work is effortless to him, because he is living his passion. It is his aim to increase the level of happiness in the world and help to improve the lives of millions of other people.

Contact information:
Please visit www.hansbeumer.com

www.ingramcontent.com/pod-product-compliance
Lightning Source LLC
LaVergne TN
LVHW091006080826
845145LV00003B/1149

9783906861050